Ten Things I Still Hate About Those Women

Twisted Love, Passion, Sisterhood and Loyalty

by

Allene E. Swienckowski

authorHOUSE®

AuthorHouse™
1663 Liberty Drive, Suite 200
Bloomington, IN 47403
www.authorhouse.com
Phone: 1-800-839-8640

This book is a work of non-fiction. Unless otherwise noted, the author and the publisher make no explicit guarantees as to the accuracy of the information contained in this book and in some cases, names of people and places have been altered to protect their privacy.

First published by AuthorHouse 7/21/2008

ISBN: 978-1-4343-1412-3 (e)
ISBN: 978-1-4343-1411-6 (sc)

Library of Congress Control Number: 2007909760

Printed in the United States of America
Bloomington, Indiana

This book is printed on acid-free paper.

Dedication:

To My Giraffe

Table of Contents

Mean, Not So Pretty Things
Chapter 1

One of the best reasons to live in southern California is soccer. The beauty of being a resident of southern California ensures that almost every soccer game will be played in brilliant sunshine from late August through March. Most games are scheduled early Saturday mornings and afternoons with a sprinkling of Sunday afternoons to even out the season. Even during those dog days of summer, the anchor of every soccer team, the soccer mom, is there to help players, coaches and referees to stave off their thirst and exhaustion. The soccer mom also bolsters the team with her generally exuberant cheering. Many soccer moms are known for their fierce competitiveness, on and off the soccer field. Most soccer moms are completely committed to their teams and most are guilty of wildly yelling from the sidelines during games at coaches from the other team, referees and of course their beloved children who are busy pursuing that elusive soccer ball down the field.

Soccer moms are also experienced carpoolers and planners of everything from Girl Scout Cookie Fundraising and Webelos to chairing and maintaining the venerable PTA. In other words, soccer moms are the pillars of most communities. Many of these moms have begun to "age gracefully" as that blush of youth fades from a once perfect figure and those once dewy cheeks now require a bit of assistance from the counters of Bobbi Brown or Laura Mercier. Most soccer moms still dress stylishly and a few may still entertain daydreams about David Beckham or some other out-of-reach hunk. Although most soccer moms are either full-time moms or are working mothers, most find ways to spend time on the soccer field several times a week with their children as a needed extension of themselves.

Most women morph into their new roles as wives and mothers easily and the price that many have to pay for this transition from youthful and vibrant beauty is typically a slight bit of weight gain around the hips and/or mid-sections of their once slender frames. But then of course there is always one woman who seems to defy the passage of time and the demands that motherhood bestows upon the rest of us. Every team of every youth sport in America has its trophy wife who just so happens to also be a goddess. A goddess is a woman who intentionally makes other women feel 'lesser than' as an entrée to a host of other negative emotions.

Our soccer goddess looks as if she tumbled out of the pages of Vogue or Elle. Everything about the goddess is perfect. She's blonde, ultra petite and her body is perfect. No flab, no wrinkles, no sag anywhere. Her breasts are also mysteriously perky even after the birth of their four children. Her bum and thighs are well-shaped and firm, a fact that is clearly displayed at every game because of her choice of crisp white shorts topped by tailored, sleeveless, and unbuttoned shirts that modestly reveals her perfect cleavage.

Our goddess arrives at the field in her new, dark blue Chevy Suburban. The goddess exits her chariot and effortlessly removes her young from their car-seats as the sun reflects off of her golden hair and glistens just like spun gold. Composed and beautiful, the goddess approaches the sidelines, flashes a flawless, perfect smile and quickly joins the most popular and powerful clique on the sidelines. The Soccer Goddess settles down with her friends as the group twitters and coos offhanded comments about "oh, your children are just adorable" and "how do you keep them so clean" to "My God, you always manage to look so great!"

These scenes of female camaraderie are faithfully played out year after year as the children grow from being young, fledgling soccer players and grow into to formidable young teenage Turks with their sights trained on the Olympics or Division One university soccer teams. Throughout these years, the goddess and I shared little more than the usual courtesy of cordial "Hello" or "How are you?" that kind of common meaningless conversation that takes place between strangers. Each of our very brief encounters was also punctuated by a hasty nod or a plastered half-smile flashed in passing. Truthfully, the Soccer Goddess had little reason to spend time with me or to engage me in a meaningful conversation. I wasn't a part of her clique. I wasn't a part of any clique for that matter, nor did I possess the credentials that would have paved the way for my acceptance into her group.

What were those unspoken entry requirements to our soccer mom clique? It would appear that the first requirement would have been physical perfection and without physical perfection then the next requirement would have been excessive wealth and or power. I possessed none of these.

The bar for top clique inclusion in our soccer club was quite high. As fate would have it, our Soccer Goddess was doubly blessed. She had managed to marry the perfect man who was a tall, darkly handsome fireman who also had gobs of money. The Soccer Goddess's beauty is so classical that she would have been admitted to the top tier popular clique solely because of her looks. Needless to say, the Soccer Goddess's children were as perfect as their parents. Mr. Goddess, even though he was drop dead gorgeous and rich, was just a regular, unpretentious guy. But one day Mr. Goddess became more than just a regular Joe. Mr. Goddess became my hero, literally.

One hot and dry day at a soccer tournament in Central CA, my son suffered a compression fracture his wrist as a result of the game. Mr. Goddess drove like a maniac to rush my son back to our local hospital at the behest of our insurance carrier who had determined that my son would receive better care at a hospital in Southern California rather than in Central California. Mr. Goddess was transformed in my heart ad soul that day and became Mr. McDreamy, my hero.

Before that nerve-racking day, I had never been invited to the Soccer Goddess's home. And that day wasn't any different except for the fact that my son had been injured and logic suggested that it was easier for me to pick him up at the Soccer Goddess's home. When I arrived at their home I was struck by the fact that this relatively young couple lived in one of the most prestigious and desired neighborhoods in the San Gabriel Valley. Their house was large, a stunning testament to

Architectural Digest. The house, like the goddess and Mr. McDreamy, was meticulously maintained with numerous adult/kid toys all stored in their assigned places. My mind flitted back over the past, idle, second-hand conversations that surmised that McDreamy had won a tidy sum in the lottery.

I managed to shake off my idle curiosity about their lifestyle and slid back into my role as chief worrier and mom. Keyed-up and stressed, I rang the doorbell. The visit began with a cool greeting from the Soccer Goddess; her manner was so cold and so distant that it was impossible not to conclude that she had decided to transform herself into the Ice Queen. She exhibited absolutely aero concern for my son and she didn't offer any of the typical "touchy feely" stuff that moms do to one another to console a mother beset by problems. Her cold stance was in stark contrast to Mr. McDreamy's intense warmth and concern. McDreamy entered and scooped me up into his powerful arms while assuring me that my son would be fine. He also assured me that it was no big deal that he had driven like a wild man. Jokingly, he stated: "The old red flashing light on the top of a car works wonders!" To make a somewhat long and uneventful story short, our son received proper medical care and he continued to play soccer after the cast was removed which took about six weeks.

Over the next few years our sons left AYSO and joined club soccer teams. So the tenuous ties that had once loosely bound us all together disintegrated. The Mc Dreamies occasionally crossed my family's path every now and again whenever our sons would play exhibition soccer games at the Rose Bowl in Pasadena, CA.

One of those days at the Rose Bowl springs instantly to mind. Game day was filled with exhilaration for the players who appreciated the opportunity to play soccer on the green expanse of the Rose Bowl that had hosted the World Cup Soccer competition a few years earlier and parents were eager to watch their sons play at a premier spot. Like the other sixteen year old boys, our son was less than ecstatic when we greeted him and his assembled teammates on our way into the stadium. As our eyes adjusted to the flash of blinding sunlight upon entering the stadium after exiting the darkened tunnel, our vision was filled quickly with the breath taking expanse of the emerald green turf. The stands close to the field were filled even though the rest of cavernous stadium yawned emptily. The immense size of the stadium was jarring because the size of the stadium was so dissimilar to the soccer fields we were all used to.

I think every person in the stands had an excellent view of the field below us. My son and his teammates juggled balls and practiced their moves until the final whistle blew to signal the end of the preceding game. Our game started in a flurry of plays between the two teams and thankfully our team forged ahead down the field towards the other team's goal post. Half-time arrived faster than I had ever remembered. Most of us were a bit giddy from the excitement of the game so my husband and I wandered out of the stands and towards the concession stands for treats. Jocularity filled the air around the concessions accompanied by the smell of grilled hot dogs and freshly popped corn.

My hubby and I exchanged idle chit chat as Mr. McDreamy suddenly appeared out of nowhere and greeted my husband with a hearty handshake and scooped me up into his arms as if he had just seen us a few days earlier. The two guys excitedly delved into the finer points of the game before Mr. McDreamy stopped and asked about our son and his future plans. During their exchange of information Mr. McDreamy saw his goddess out of the corner of his eye. Even though five years had passed, the Soccer Goddess was as beautiful as ever; maybe even more so because it seemed as if she hadn't aged one tiny bit over the last few years. Excitedly, McDreamy turned towards his wife and boomed: "He honey look, its Josh's parents!" As our son's name fell on the tiny perfect ears of the Soccer Goddess and recognition dawned, the muscles in her face tightened and her once beautiful, flawless face turned dark and sour. I dismissed the look on her face and assumed that her dour expression had more to do with something nearby that smelled unpleasant as it leaked from one of the concessions or from a nearby trash bin.

My husband and I smiled the obligatory smile and waved the obligatory wave and mouthed our "Hellos!" Although I had never been a friend to the Soccer Goddess I had always admired her stellar beauty and her story-book lifestyle. The Soccer Goddess had always represented to me what most of normal females would call the "ultimate dream." Like most women, I fantasize about the usual: the perfect home, the perfect man (I have the perfect man) coupled with enough time and money to enjoy and experience life together. In my eyes, the Soccer Goddess and McDreamy lived "the dream." From my vantage point which was located from the outside of their lives peering in, the Soccer Goddess's life seemed just perfect in every way. Truthfully, I slept a little better at night knowing that someone I knew lived very well without worry or stress. I had never tried to cultivate a relationship with the Soccer Goddess or Mr. McDreamy because I was so keenly aware that we had so very little in common. Our only connection was our sons and they no longer played soccer together, on the same teams.

Whatever happens between people in life, that is the unspoken things, was clearly at work on that sunny day at the Rose Bowl in Pasadena California. Unfortunately, whatever unexplained phenomenon happened resulted in me ending up being in one of the most uncomfortable social situations of my life. Unbidden, the situation unfolded bizarrely before me. It quickly became clear that the Soccer Goddess hadn't detected a foul smell in the air that had caused her fine features to contort into a scowl. It was painfully obvious that what had disturbed her perfect features was the presence of me and my husband. The Soccer Goddess's tightly clenched jaws apparently rendered her speechless but once they were unclenched, she simply refused to speak to us. Her greeting was an intense glare punctuated by sparks of unspoken molten hatred. Her silence cut through lively bubble of activity around us like a sharp, hot knife gliding through butter. The silence between us became tangible and imploded outward like a shockwave through the once giddy crowd that surrounded us. The air seemed to compress around us. The suck of silence was so intense that my husband and I could only muster slight facial twitches in response to her rebuff much like the involuntary twitches of horse flanks under attack by a swarm of hungry flies.

It was clear that the Soccer Goddess was angry and had decided to be consciously rude. Silence as a tactic is normally considered rude by civilized people and is typically employed by women when they are angry and understand that the power of their silence works best when directed against a spouse or a child. This classic feminine response almost always results in the victim feeling total shame and embarrassment simply because of the classic silent treatment. Most women have learned the art of how to inflict emotional pain and embarrassment upon others. For a whole lot of people, to have a woman, any woman to glare silently at them, is the ultimate non-verbal slap in the face.

The Soccer Goddess's blatant rudeness was particularly uncalled for because our relationship up until that moment had essentially been non-existent and decidedly socially acceptable because it was merely a surface relationship. The Soccer Goddess and I weren't even like two ships passing in the dark of night because we just passed one another without even making a wake in each other's lives. For me, the rebuff from the Soccer Goddess that day was like being slapped, a physical action that is always emotionally jarring and demeaning. I was stunned to the point of being speechless and being speechless for me is a very rare occurrence. The initial shock quickly turned into embarrassment. My emotions shifted into overdrive and every slight that I had ever suffered in my entire lifetime because of mean girls and mean women rocketed to the surface as my cheeks began to prickle with rage. My anger kicked into full throttle as the realization became clear that the Soccer Goddess intended to wound me emotionally. My brain sang crazily – Newsflash Dummy: The Soccer Goddess is one of the many mean girls who grew-up and comfortably remains in her role of being a mean girl, even after she was supposed to be all grown-up! It became suddenly clear to me that the Soccer Goddess and I were both doomed – she as a throwback mean girl in middle school and me as the person who had never recovered from my experiences with mean girls.

It was obvious that the Soccer Goddess was very comfortable being one of the not-so-pretty-mean-things that flourish very well in Western cultures. Little girl bullies bud in elementary school and are officially identified as "mean girls" by other little girls long before they reach middle school. Mean girls, or girl bullies, are unlike boy bullies because these girls spend their early school years cultivating and practicing how to emotionally maim and /or manipulate others. The initial targets of this brand of girl meanness are typically other little girls who are deemed socially unacceptable or unlikable by budding mean girls.

Each and every girl/woman who is older than twelve has personally experienced the oft times veiled and manipulative emotional attacks by other women. Typically, these types of emotional assaults are launched by a group of mean girls who are also, inexplicably, the popular trend setters on most middle and high school campuses. The female talk shows and female magazines rarely if ever address the fact that "mean girls" grow-up and become mean women. For the most part, these talk shows and magazines are filled with stories of women conquering the glass ceiling in corporate America or being successful entrepreneurs. Unfortunately, there are not a lot of successful women reaching down to embrace and mentor groups of younger women who hunger for success and need their help.

But what about "those women" that make other women squirm in their own skins? "Those women" are the goddess/divas that cause other women to walk away from all encounters with goddesses because these women always walk away with feeling "less than." These grown-up mean girls are masters at robbing others of their self-confidence, esteem and sometimes even their self worth. "Those women" are expert deconstructors because they thrive on belittling and demeaning other human beings.

I'm certain that many of you who managed to survive puberty and became self- sufficient individuals still remember the encounters you've had with the "mean girls" who matured into mean women? If you were one of the lucky ones, maybe the last time you came into personal contact with a mean girl was in middle or high school. But if you're like the rest of us, that is, the vast sea of non-goddesses, then your adult lives has been plagued by mean women masquerading as normal compassionate women.

Most of us will never forget that first sting of rejection that we experienced from a group of three or four little girls; typically all huddled together on the playground or in the cafeteria and made it crystal clear that you weren't "good enough" to be a part of their clique. Ah, we can all remember what it felt like when we were targeted by one of the goddess cliques; that awful sound of their giggling at you interspersed with their humiliating taunts that echoed and reverberated throughout the quad and out bodies as the whole groups attention shifted towards you, the target for the day.

Of course the victim found it impossible to escape from their imperious gazes. Only pure will-power could force the victim to either hang their head in shame or to try to scuttle away from the attack, all in the hope of avoiding feeling like an insignificant, cockroach. On the other hand, the victim might have come from defiant stock and therefore managed to throw her shoulders and head back while focusing on an unseen spot on far wall across the abyss while determinedly striding past that group of mean girls without so much as a glance in their direction. Regardless of her response to the emotional assault, the victim is dying from a terminal case of shame that burns her cheeks, stings her eyes and wounds her soul.

As a pre-teen girl, this type of encounter with a mean girl was so emotionally profound that involuntary physical responses take control of the body. Pre-teen girls reflexively reach to smooth or straighten their hair and once assured that the hair is in place that same hand darts quickly over their clothing as the hand tugs and pulls nervously at a skirt or smoothes a blouse in response to an attack about her appearance from the mean girls. The victim's heart begins to pound thunderously as the deafening sound of her rushing blood fills her ears and roars like a locomotive as she searches desperately for a way to project an image of self-confidence in front of the mean girls. At the very least the victim would simply like for the clique to think that she was a "nice girl." The victim prays silently for the tormentors to stop looking at and tormenting her. Instead, the mean girls escalate their attack and begin to whisper, audibly, about the victim's so-called offensive faults or habits. "I mean like, isn't her hair pathetic?" "Look at her dirty shoes?" "Where did she get that outfit, at the Goodwill?" Collective, raucous laughter sounds like a death knell to the victim as their mocking escalates and she plummets emotionally while the mean girls sharpen their talons in preparation for a renewed assault.

The victim always tries to conjure a calamity to strike instantly that miraculously destroys everyone within sight. But of course no disaster miraculously occurs and the abuse from the mean girls continues and the victim's shame spirals. For the victim, time has shifted into slow and for some bizarre reason it suddenly takes forever to just to walk across the quad, a walk that was no more than a hop, skip and a jump. The victim always wonders about what possibly could it be that makes her so hated by the mean girl clique?

Of course no one avoids remembering these types of awful encounters when the color rose in their cheeks as the sting of hot tears welled behind their eyes because of that kind of rejection and shame. And there is nothing worse than that awful, gnawing pain of rejection; a stigma that never leaves your soul even as you age and mature. But today, as a grown woman you are cast once again as a student in middle school. You are the victim who struggles to walk safely by the mean girl clique without stumbling or making a fool of yourself. The sub-teen goddess in training always smirk and taunt other girls, her mouth filled with venom and derision rarely experiences what they dish out so freely to others. Sadly, the collective mind weave and voices of the mean girls continue to sear the flesh of their victims like acid even today as each generation produces its own band of mean girls and mean women.

The Soccer Goddess opened up all these submerged wounds that I had suffered over the years from far too many not so pretty mean things on that sunny, hot day at the Rose Bowl. The perfect Soccer Goddess revealed that she was a shrew right in front of strangers and her man. Her once beautiful, tranquil face became a disfigured and contorted, immobile mask of anger. McDreamy tried to simultaneously brush aside his bafflement and surprise at his perfect wife's unexpected behavior. But Mr. McDreamy was out of his league because he just couldn't understand his wife's out-of-character behavior towards us. Mr. McDreamy then reached reflexively for his Soccer Goddess and when he made contact with her flesh he began to massage her stiff shoulders while trying to coax her into being cordial. The Soccer Goddess wrenched her shoulders from his grasp and stomped off like a disgruntled child. McDreamy attempted to push aside the very volatile situation that was building before his eyes as he attempted, one last time, to get his goddess to say "Hello." McDreamy physically interrupted her forward momentum and halted her departure in mid-stride.

The tension in the small space surrounding us was so intense that strangers began to move out of line and away from the coming calamity. The skin on my face prickled because of the insult and the intensity of the situation. I struggled trying not to respond to this situation as if I was still that scorned eight year old girl, caught up in the past. I tried valiantly to "suck it up" because I really wanted to respond to her and the uncomfortable situation that she had placed us all in without cause. I wanted to respond to the situation as if I was a functioning adult who was unmoved by her rejection. I was vulnerable and for some obscure reason I believe that I wasn't "good enough" for the Soccer Goddess to even have the decency to say "Hello."

In a last ditch attempt, McDreamy reached for and gently shook his Soccer Goddess by the shoulders and demanded to: "Say Hello! Don't be so cold and rude, honey!" The tiny, perfect Soccer Goddess firmly planted her tiny feet on the ground and glared at him in the way that only wives can glare at their husbands when they've made-up their minds not to budge on an issue. The Soccer Goddess pulled away violently from McDreamy's grasp and stomped off leaving him alone and confused. The battle was over – a battle that McDreamy was not even aware of was taking place. There was absolutely nothing that McDreamy could say or do to make his Soccer Goddess speak to us.

My husband and I returned silently to our seats and watched the end of the game in silence and then we walked back to our car consumed with a different type of silence. Over the years my husband and I have discussed the incident and neither one of us can understand what had caused the Soccer Goddess to publicly insult us. It was extremely clear to us that we had offended the Soccer Goddess in some unknown way and yet whatever had catapulted us into that social quagmire has never been revealed.

Historically, women of every social class and race have exercised this particularly feminine trait of condemnation: the absolute cruelty of seething silence. These quiet, emotional storms that women experience generally cause everyone else near these miffed goddesses to hop around while trying to pacify and mollify them, regardless of whether or not the woman/goddess has been the instigator of the situation. Little girls who are destined to grow-up and become mean girls learn how to effectively use their anger and displeasure against others from either their mothers or other powerful women in their lives.

The talent of being a manipulator is passed from mother to daughter just as surely as genetic traits such as blue eyes and blond hair are passed from generation to generation. All little kids play make-believe and mimic the actions and the emotional responses of their care-givers. Little girls play and pretend to be "grown-up mommy" and wear their mothers' high heels, dresses and hats while little boys don their father's suits, shoes and hats. Emotionally alive, little girls closely observe, copy and ingest the emotional network of the people around them whether or not those emotions are good, bad or manipulative. Little girls will be inclined to mimic the emotional patterns of the people in their lives that make them feel safe and secure. Hence, some little girls grow-up to exert their learned emotional prowess against others while exacting emotional payback from the people in their lives because these girls have learned the power that comes with self-confidence whereas little boys learn to exert their physical power against others.

A rough-cut of history reveals that a woman's role for centuries has been to simply raise the progeny and to maintain a functioning household while the husbands and/or their fathers were expected to conquer continents and extend and expand their personal power and wealth. Women over the centuries had to develop emotional responses to quell negative behaviors in their children and at times, other women in their lives and their social realm. And on occasion some women have also had to subtly check the negative behavior of their husbands by effectively using their well-honed emotions often laced with poisoned words when the silent technique failed to yield the desired behavior. Most mean little girls master the art of emotional manipulation to gain power over other little girls by the time they enter elementary school. These little darlings have learned the topography of petty jealousy or the art of being an emotional care-giver and many young girls make unconscious decisions to make sure that someone other than themselves will become the emotional victim. Mean girls grow-up to be adult goddesses and feel that they are entitled to exhibit and practice trash behavior to the world at large or to re-invent the truth in order to further their own agendas whether or not their actions are harmful or hurtful to others or not.

The Soccer Goddess obviously felt that she was entitled to insult and withhold common courtesy because she had decided that we were undesirable. The Soccer Goddess felt no obligation to honor the social contract that had functioned in the past therefore it became acceptable for her to socially snub us. Unfortunately, the armor that I had spent many years constructing against such social rejections developed a gaping hole.

After emotional numbness came anger. I became angry for many reasons; the least of which was that I allowed a petty, mean woman to make me feel "less than." I had refused to admit that I could still be made to feel "less than" by another woman since I'd matured into an adult. The brief, venomous sting of rejection from the Soccer Goddess resurrected a tidal wave of all the previous times that I had been rejected by other little girls and women throughout my lifetime.

I responded to the situation in an almost civilized fashion by composing a letter to the Soccer Goddess. I chose to ignore and not mention all of the negativity the goddess had resurrected that had slumbered deep inside of me, unmolested for many, many years. The letter stated simply that once upon a time I had admired her, even though I didn't really know her as a person. I reminded her of her petty behavior at the Rose Bowl and that her behavior should have been beneath a woman of her stature in the community. I told her that she didn't know me or my husband well enough to have sunk to such a low level of social impropriety or to simply decide that we weren't worthy enough to extend a "Hello."

I completed the short, brief letter to the Southern CA Soccer Goddess with what I thought was an appropriate aphorism: "To those that much is given, much is expected."

Undying, Unquestioning Allegiance
Chapter 2

Almost everyone over the age of thirty has said at least once that the best days of their lives were the ones they spent in high school. The truth is, those statements have been found to be more propaganda than truth. If past recollections can be accepted as accurate, then it might become possible to determine if the statement about an enjoyable time in high school is either fact or fiction. How many times have you personally heard a high school student say: "This is the best time of my life!"? The truth is that old people, that are people over thirty, invented the lie to share with their children in the hope that their children would complete high school without too much trauma. The sad reality is that old folks know that life in high school for most students is a life chocked full of woes and foes. Anyone who attended high school has also experienced a lot of unpleasant memories. The short version of most people's experience is an emphatic: "It Sucked!"

High school sucked for almost everyone. Although it's hard to believe but high school sucked for the jocks, the prom queens, the cheerleaders as well as the nerds. . In other words, high school sucked for almost everyone and that includes teachers and administrators. Just think about having to deal with the vagaries of teenage boys and girls' day in and day out, except that you're an adult. Now that really **SUCKS**, right?

High school, for most students, is a modern day horror story. Every kid older than thirteen has received sentence that requires them to serve three or four years in their local high school. The sentence is generally punitive for most kids. Everyday begins at some preset, ungodly hour in the morning, for a minimum of 200 days a year. To add insult to injury, students are also required to master incomprehensible courses in math, science and English in addition to being a part of that social chaos that is the foundation for all high school encounters.

To most students, trudging daily through the hallways of their local high school took unimaginable courage. Might we hasten to once again trek down those dark and foreboding hallways to simply recall those days that were characterized by the endless rows of lockers on either the side of those gleaming, newly waxed floors at the beginning of the beginning of every school year that quickly degenerated into a trash-strewn wasteland. Of course those memories still haunt us all, which in part compels most of us to attend the ten year high school reunion where everyone is curious to see what Joe Jock and Molly Prom Queen grew-up to be.

However, while you were in high school you reminded yourself that once you graduated you would be an adult; whatever that means. Whatever! The task required you to brave what happened in the hallways, the cafeteria, the quad and that most dreaded of placed, the gym. A staggering number of high school graduates can quickly and accurately recall their personalized agony experienced in high school. This negative video encased in the brain pan is a testament to the days spent in high school and to the fact that those days will never be known as: "The Best Days of My Life."

So, while high school is truly a social wasteland for a lot of students, it is also the breeding ground and birthplace for those emotionally toxic relationships – the clique. Many of these female cliques eventually morph into adult female groups of exclusivity and become known to other women as the goddess/diva class.

To some observers it might appear that female cliques mysteriously arise within all high school communities. But many cliques were formed in middle school. Cliques function mainly to largely give their members emotional security. Security is found because the members typically share at least one thing in common whether it be looks, academic acumen, or social power.

In our society, physical appearance is extremely important and more so for women. Unfortunately, I've never met a woman who was totally satisfied with her looks or her body. Acceptance of her physical image is even more difficult for women today because most women's real world is saturated with air brushed and/or digitized perfected females. The overall effect has been that for the most part, a large percentage of women never feel quite beautiful or perfect enough. And these feelings persist despite the fact that fathers, husbands and lovers of all types tell women that they are perfect in their eyes. These types of compliments from men or even other women are typically swished away by most women as if the complement was an annoying fly flitting around their face.

Most women learned this specific emotional response that is to reject all complements about ones physicality, in high school. High school is the place where sex becomes a major issue to all young people. Although many girls in high school pass muster for being attractive few are sexy. High school is the place where young girls acquire and hone what they consider to be their sexual allure, and for some, high school is the place where they learn to avoid the issue of sex altogether. The pressures of high school make every student want to escape that place that is littered with landmines. Every high school student dreams of leaving high school and leaving the clique mentality behind.

So, going off to college is supposed to fix all of those sticky social problems encountered in high school, right? Wrong!

College is the place where everyone is all grown-up. In college there are no cliques and no petty rivalries. College is a place where students go to figure out who they are and lead a life filled with purpose and loads of fun. But in the back drop for many high school graduates is the realization that college is just a continuation of that anxiety and pain one encountered while in high school. In other words, college turns out to be a mix of all of those awful social situations experienced in high school, but with the added benefit of too much alcohol to make the situation worse. Every college freshman approaches their new life in college with butterflies in their stomachs despite that faint promise that college is going to be a liberating experience.

For many high school grads, move-in day arrives and yet most are still immature and unready for college. The transition begins gradually with the college student and their parents lugging boxes up flights of stairs and into rooms where they'll live with total strangers. The intuitive, almost adult new college student easily recognizes the strain behind mom's eyes and the pride in dad's smile. Most students manage to ignore the pain behind mom's eyes because most are afraid that they too might break-down and cry. And how grown-up is a blubbering baby who's crying simply because their mommy is leaving them behind? Of course there are a few wet eyes here and there on the campus on move-in day but most students and a lot of parents do in fact manage to not cry!

To cut down on external social pressures at college, some students choose to attend colleges that don't have sororities or fraternities. As it turns out, the lure of Greek Life is very similar to high school cliques. For students who aspire to join frats and sororities the exhaustive process of pledging and the exclusivity of acceptance into these organizations is sometimes a guarantee that these new college students will experience a lot more broken egos and hearts, just like in high school. But on move-in day the campus, checking-in, and parents leaving is generally too much for most new freshmen.

To add to the tension there are three roommates to share one tiny room. They begin to unpack. The inadequate and small space to be shared by the three roommates is amicably divvied up. Each roommate tries, in their own way, to adjust to the small, cramped but quaint living quarters that they will share for the next academic school year. For most girls living in small, unfamiliar circumstances it takes about two weeks for the engrained, polite manners to wear thin to be replaced by natural tensions that arise and erupt between women who have absolutely nothing in common. It took less than the typical two weeks for the tension to rise between myself and my new roommates.

Upon reflection, the tension with my roommates actually began on move-in day. Apparently, I had over-steeped my boundaries by claiming the best space in the cramped room. I managed to arrive at college bright and early on move-in day. The Residential Life Team met me on my arrival and a phalanx of helpful dorm fellows helped move my humongous load of possessions into my new dorm room. My dorm fellow was a friendly brunette. She told me that I could choose where I wanted to place my bed and desk since I arrived first.

My second roommate arrived about an hour later. After the initial introductions we discussed how to improve on what was obviously a cramped, and at the moment, very ugly living space. Three hours later the third roommate arrived to find that by arriving late that she had forfeited her opportunity to choose where to put her bed and desk. The second and third roommates inherited a bunk bed because the room was too small to accommodate three twin beds.

From the moment that the Late Goddess arrived, she was standoffish and unfriendly. Upon entering the room, the almost attractive, petite, redhead looked around with a scowl that blanketed her fine features with obvious dissatisfaction. Ms. Late Goddess also had quite a unique relationship with her parents. The goddess snapped commands at her mom and dad as she spewed a constant flow of dissatisfaction at her quiescent, obedient parents. Her tones were so biting and cold that it was impossible for the rest of us in the room not to flinch and squirm uncomfortably because of her unbridled assault. For what seemed like an eternity Ms. Late Goddess spewed a continuous stream of disappointment, dissatisfaction and resentment at her parents. I couldn't help but to think that the two would, for the first time in years, experience peace in their home.

Ms. Late Goddess barely acknowledged us. As the tension mounted, Ms. Late Goddess determined that her two new roommates were docile and apparently compliant, like her parents. She made her move and made it quite clear that she felt that she was entitled to the best spot in the room. Ms. Late Goddess's apparent entitlement arose from the fact that she had been raised to believe that she was entitled; well just because! Ms. Late Goddess was extremely secure in the belief that she was special and therefore entitled while everyone else was not special and therefore was supposed to grant her every whim. After a few hours of exposure to Ms. Late Goddess and her flagrant attitude, it was clear that she should be renamed: Ms. Privileged.

Ms. Privileged arrived at college, like the rest of us without an established core group. But Ms Privileged was so used to being in "charge" of other girls that she was able to make quick emotional inroads with roommate number two. Roommate number two accepted Ms. Privileged as top goddess and she also convinced our dorm fellow that she was "all that" and as such deserved special treatment. My other roommate, herein after to be called Ms. Cling because of her need to belong to a group. Ms. Cling and I were closer in attitude and temperament but Ms. Privileged appealed to Ms. Cling's keen desire to be included in a group. It just so happens that while the two girls began to fall in league with one another, Ms. Privileged made sure that she and Ms. Cling avoided contact with me. Her philosophy was based on "divide and conquer." Their contact with me was largely mean and nasty. So for me, as in high school, college became a social wasteland. It was bad enough that my home and friends were a mere three thousand miles away, but in less than thirty days after my arrival it became abundantly clear that I lived with two mean girl clones who were capable of perpetrating unspeakable acts of cruelty.

Within a few weeks Ms. Privileged reached out to a group of other goddesses on campus and established her core clique. On one bright sunny day before the days of frigid winter descended, Ms. Privileged actually took the time to speak at me. She always spoke "at" me rather than to me because she clearly didn't think that I was high enough on the scale to be considered another human being. The only reason Ms. Privileged spoke to me was because she felt an obligation to inform me as to "why" she disliked me so much. The scene unfolded like some dumb teen movie about college life.

Ms. Privileged was idly sprawled on the top bunk that she shared with Ms. Cling. I felt like I had been caught by my mother with my hand in the cookie jar BEFORE dinner. Ms. Privileged was eyeing me like I was her afternoon snack and she now only slightly resembled the pixie cute girl who had insulted her parents and ignored Ms. Cling and I on move-in day. Dark clouds actually formed overhead outside in the sky and part of that spreading gloom was transported into our dorm room. The descending darkness outside from the gathering storm coalesced with her once angelic, pixie face. Before she spoke, her tiny frame heaved dramatically as her head jerked to and fro eerily in sync with her emotion. Then the words spewed: "I mean, you're like so ridiculous! How could you come to college with your high school boyfriend? You are stupid and juvenile and until you decide to sever your relationship with "it," I'll make sure that your life here is a living hell." Although I was taken aback by her attack, I was finally able to make sense of what she was saying. It became 'oh so' impossible for me not to burst out laughing in her face.

Ms. Privileged had managed to create a minor stir in our entire dorm in just a few short weeks simply because she objected to my relationship with my high school sweetheart. To hasten my social demise on campus,

Ms. Privileged began to spread malicious rumors and lies about me around campus. When Ms. Privileged wasn't spreading rumors about me she was busy sure that she would be remembered as the campus punch board. She seemed to prefer transient, tawdry and noisy one night stands.

After the sting of her rejection began to wane, I was able to giggle about the fact that my committed relationship was the thorn in the side of the resident "Girls Gone Wild" mascot. What chutzpah Ms. Privileged had; damning me simply because she didn't like the fact that I was involved in a long-term relationship. Perhaps if Ms. Privileged hadn't undertaken the task of being the campus poster child for the absurd, I might have taken the time to try to talk to her like she was a rational human being. As it was, Ms. Privileged spent quite a lot of time poisoning other people's minds about who I was and why they should disassociate themselves from me.

Since Ms. Privileged's observations and advice produced no noticeable change in my behavior, believe it or not my social value plummeted on campus like a boulder that had been thrown down the side of a mountain. I became the object of hatred and scorn in my dorm in less than a month. I knee-deep in studying most of my waking hours therefore I was completely unaware that my social life was quickly turning into the Twilight Zone. The first real consequence to happen, personally, was that it became literally impossible for me to study in my own dorm room; ever. Both roommates had a constant flow of visitors who were generally loud, disruptive, and drunk. It became crystal clear that neither of my two roommates needed as much time to study as I did simply because neither chose to study. I learned that if I wanted to study I had to relocate and study in other places like library that was just a mere ten minute jaunt from our dorm room in the sleet and snow, or in the dorm's very public parlor.

In an attempt to keep an even keel while I was under attack, I had to quickly acquire skills that would ensure me the peace of mind that I could avoid all contact with them. The sad truth: I actually got along with and related better to my boyfriend's roommates than I did with Ms. Privileged and Ms. Cling. I was literally adopted by my boyfriend's roommates and they allowed me to come and go as I pleased at any hour of the day or night.

For all of you readers who may assume that my non-response to and avoidance of my roommates was wimpy? Well, think again! If you come up with "whiney and spineless" please scroll back through your own pasts and think about all of the compromises that you had to make over your lifetimes just to keep the peace with other women. The expert tongue-biting that you've practiced over the years just to live your life peacefully without having to look over shoulder out of fear is exactly what I was attempting. We all hope to find that magic door of sisterhood, the one you've dreamed about and heard about on Oprah or Ellen. Experience speaks volumes and my avoidance tactic didn't free me from their attacks nor did my plan bring me peace. As most of you women may have guessed from your own personal experiences with other women over the years, my problems only escalated and devolved into an untenable situation. The feud I never sought blew-up and became a dorm-wide donnybrook.

My social life, although miniscule, soon degenerated into being much less, as if that was even possible. I couldn't avoid feeling like I was being dipped into a cauldron of hot boiling oil. The only communication that could occur between Ms. Privileged, Ms. Cling and I was caustic and their brief conversations with me were always peppered with barbs and innuendo. Ms. Privileged was obviously the power goddess because she was clearly able to sway the emotions of others even though what she said was a pack of lies. No matter, the thing to understand about this dynamic is that the role of a goddess acolyte is to obey the power goddess regardless of whether the mission of the power goddess is just or not. Acolytes rarely, if ever, question the motives of the power goddess because questioning her desires almost always results in some form of punishment for the questioning acolyte. Punishment ranges between expulsion from the clique to ridicule. On the other hand, the power goddess might decide to maintain the errant acolyte in her clique in order to use the acolyte as her personal scratching post. Although I had to learn how to avoid both roommates like the plague, I was also aware of the fact the Ms. Cling was obviously emotionally challenged and that she was incapable of being able to withstand the negative emotional climate that Ms. Privileged dispensed. And as for Ms. Cling the underling, her position mandated that she could never question the motives of Ms. Privileged.

I was a persona non-grata in my own room and the situation worsened as strangers were invited into our room by my roommates and allowed to lounge on my bed, invade my personal space, or to use my goods/products without permission. As the end of the semester approached and Winter Break loomed, the emotional situation in the room became untenable. While home for the holidays I decided that I couldn't stomach another day living with people who had no more use for me than a used tissue so it became imperative for me to request a dorm transfer. Even after I moved-out of the small, cramped room, Ms. Privileged continued to spread vicious lies about me to people who didn't even know me.

So, the question becomes; just what is it with some women who feel it is absolutely okay to trash other women? And why is it that other women who are perfectly capable of forming their own opinions, decide to emotionally bankrupt people at the request of another woman? The answer to these not so lofty questions is that many people, and especially women, don't mind having other people to tell them what to think or how to live their lives.

But wait! My personal college saga with the goddess class continued. After I returned from Winter Break I moved in with a new roommate. This new roommate was a treasure; because of her sweet and helpful personality her name will be La Saint. To put it simply, La Saint was everything my other two roommates weren't. First of all La Saint was a human being but she was also kind, caring, and a dedicated student. La Saint was actively involved in campus issues such as recycling. La Saint helped me to heal my bruised ego and after a while I began to develop a social network.

During the course of my resurrection I also met a few other new people who I thought were nice and humane. I toyed with the idea that one or two of these people might become, in the future of course, friends. I was attracted to this new group because they seemed, on the surface, to be like my friend group from high school; that is kind of nerdy but nice. Oh…what a twisted web I had begun to weave. I mean, just how wrong could I have been? Again? Apparently, I would find out all too soon that I was very, very wrong about how to judge others character. My faux pas was so great this time that I graduated from being wrong to criminally negligent. Even after being exposed to La Saint and her splendid qualities, I apparently hadn't learned to be a good judge of people and their motivations.

Now enter Ms. Princess Goddess and Mr. Sir In/Out of the Closet. Ms. Princess Goddess was also petite and perky like Ms. Privileged. The similarity between the two should have been warning clue number one for me. But Ms. Princess Goddess was really cute, a brunette with a vibrant and wicked sense of humor. Sir In/Out of the Closet was tall, pale and boyish with mounds of curly, unkempt brown curls. On the surface, the Princess Goddess and Sir In/Out of the Closet seemed to be a perfect match for one another. After spending my first semester in college caught in a social nightmare, my friendly new roommate and a new group of friends seemed to mean that life had settled down for me and that I could expect normalcy in my social life.

So, new friendships began to gel just before Spring Break with Sir In/Out of the Closet and the Princess Goddess. Before the week of finals things got even rosier for the Princess and Sir In/Out of the Closet. They officially became a couple. The Princess Goddess was ecstatic and Sir In/Out of the Closet began to brood as a curtain of gloom fell over his entire existence. Oddly, as the school year ended the new couple barely progressed beyond hand holding. The strange thing about the change in their relationship was that they had actually been a lot more physical with one another before they became a couple. Their previous behavior towards one another was more like they were siblings. Before becoming a couple they had frequently rough-housed and wrestled with one another. The change in behavior of the two was in stark contrast to their previous, full of life, fun-loving attitudes in the past.

The summer began as the Princess Goddess returned to her native southern hometown before she winged off to a European summer internship. Sir In/Out of the Closet returned home and worked in a chemical plant to earn money for his tuition and pocket change. Sir In/Out of the Closet took the opportunity of distance between the two to avoid all kinds of communication with the Princess Goddess during the summer. On the other hand, he managed to maintain communication with me and my boyfriend even though we were three thousand miles away. The truth was, Mr. In/Out of the Closet felt that he was under attack. the Princess Goddess sent numerous e-mails and unending cell phone messages to him; all of which he ignored. Sir In/Out of the Closet felt that the Princess Goddess had turned into a stalker. Never mind that he chose to ignore her and made no attempt to explain his change of heart to her. Fueled by insecurity and fear, the Princess Goddess became even more insistent in her attempts to make Mr. In/Out of the Closet contact her. Mr. In/Out of the Closet felt like a trapped animal and became even more sullen.

The truth of the situation was that Sir In/Out of the Closet was caught in a life altering struggle. He had managed to avoid this very personal struggle since he had been an adolescent in middle school. Sir In/Out of the Closet had spent most of puberty not being attracted to girls. He had never allowed himself to think about being attracted to other boys. He knew that if he had allowed himself to think about being attracted to boys that he would be ostracized by everyone in his life. The thought of losing his support network convinced him to ignore his natural feelings. So, he spent his adolescent years emotionally numbed and unable to grapple with the issues of sex.

The summer of self-reflection yielded loads of information to Sir In/Out of the Closet and he understood, clearly, that he was without sexual feelings for the Princess Goddess. This solitary revelation allowed him to begin to understand himself. This understanding also led him to a painful reality that he was still reluctant to embrace – he was gay. Initially, the reality of his homosexuality shamed and repulsed him. Trapped and extremely unhappy, Sir In/Out of the Closet realized that he was going to have to tell his family. He hoped that his parents understood that he had never really liked girls in "that way" in his entire life. It also became clear to him why he avoided establishing a relationship with the Princess Goddess.

At some point during the summer the two decided that they didn't want to speak to one another. Once the 'relationship' had ended for the two they decided to appoint me to be their official intermediary. Despite this decision, Mr. In/Out of the Closet decided to send an e-mail to the Princess Goddess, an official notice that he had to sever their relationship. The decent part of him decided that he should also include in the note that he wanted the two of them to remain friends adding that he could never see the two of them being more than friends. To be fair, the Princess Goddess perceived the "good-bye" e-mail as the ultimate rejection. Not only was she rejected but she also felt that he had insulted her. The perceived insult was reason enough for the Princess Goddess to wage an all out war against Mr. In/Out of the Closet.

Of course rejection of any type to most people is always translated into the feeling that they aren't "good enough." Rejection by someone who also happens to be an object of desire is a very painful experience for almost everyone. Some women take being rejected by their significant other as if they had lost a limb or a close loved one. For a lot of women, even in today's liberal climate, being rejected by a desired male is one of the big one's and many women never learn how to cope with that type of rejection. Consequently, many women believe that being rejected by a man is a lot more serious than when a woman rejects a man. The reality is that both men and women experience emotional pain when either is rejected by their desired object.

The Princess Goddess didn't respond any differently than a lot of women to being dumped by Mr. In/Out of the Closet.. At first she reacted with tears followed by wailing and the wailing increased significantly, particularly in volume. Her pain quickly turned into wrath and allowed her to hatch a plan that she thought would emotionally annihilate Mr. In/Out of the Closet.

Her plan began like so many other mean-spirited plans that are generally only spearheaded by goddesses. The Princess Goddess initiated her plan by tearfully re-telling each one of her friends about how she had been dumped by Mr. In/Out of the Closet. Collectively, each girl felt the Princess Goddess's pain and each girl decided to sabotage Mr. In/Out of the Closet whenever the opportunity presented itself. All female members of that clique knew that the Princess Goddess had to make Mr. In/Out of the Closet pay for his sin and because they all supported her, each clique member agreed to do her fair share in making Mr. In/Out of the Closet suffer some great humiliation and/or pain. The Princess Goddess was an emotional wreck and the only time that she appeared to regain composure was when she and her friends were planning their attack against Mr. In/Out of the Closet. In their twisted sisterhood, the Princess Goddess and her friends agreed to inflict emotional pain against another human being for the sin of breaking the heart of the Princess Goddess. . Not only did he break the Princess Goddess's heart but he had also shamed her. So, for this clique, it became clear that they had to engineer a carefully thought out plan that would result in great suffering for Mr. In/Out of the Closet.

The powwow of the Sisterhood of the Casted Aside always coalesced with tears and sobs that were promptly followed by molten hot lava emotions conjured to launch towards a hated object. The heat of their combined their emotions always bonded each goddess to the cause. To that assembled group of goddesses, all men were heartless ingrates and deserved no mercy from any female for any reason. As the emotional net casted by the Princess Goddess grew it produced a battle-ready army of females' intent on exacting at least a pound of flesh from the offensive male. My part in the rising passion play remained unknown and unstated. For the moment, I tried to escape from their unleashed wrath because I didn't support her campaign against Mr. In/Out of the Closet.

You see, being a woman requires, no, demands that female friends and acquaintances break-off all contact with anyone they dislike and that includes all communication with one of their ex's. Every loyal friend of the goddess must not only commiserate with her during her hour of bereavement but all of her female friends are expected to seek and enact revenge against the ex. In the case of Sir In/Out of the Closet, overnight he became a greatly hated entity by a group of at least ten young collegian women.

In the real world of college life, the mix of all of this free floating hatred ensnared me, as well. I wasn't caught up in the melee as a participant in the lynch mob hunting for Mr. Sir In/Out of the Closet, but because I was a hated betrayer of the Princess Goddess because I had simply chosen to stay out of the fray. I also unwittingly became a target of the the the Princess Goddess's Man Haters assassination committee because I chose to remain friends with Mr. In/Out of the Closet despite his lost social standing with the Princess Goddess and her clan. Now, in the world of women, if a 'sister' decides to remain neutral in such a situation, her decision is considered an act of treason against all other women as well. If you doubt for a moment how serious and real this emotional response is in women you have only to look at how many women attacked and vilified Hillary Rodham Clinton after she decided to forgive Bill after his affair with Monica Lewinsky.

No, it didn't matter to the Princess Goddess and her cadre of unquestioning, motivated henchwomen that Mr. In/Out of the Closet was being as honest as he could have been, at the time, with the Princess Goddess about his feelings. The only thing that mattered to the Princess Goddess and her cadre was that the goddess had been maligned and insulted by Mr. In/Out of the Closet; therefore and henceforth forever, Mr. In/Out of the Closet deserved ill will and ill treatment from the Princess Goddess and every female who claimed to be a friend to the Princess Goddess.

As surely as the earth gently turns on its axis, people, things, and circumstances change. Mr. In/Out of the Closet was somewhat torn and confused by his recent epiphany and that epiphany also represented a major problem for him being able to tell his father about his new status as a gay man. Mr. In/Out of the closet was quite certain that he wasn't attracted to women. So, after taking the summer to consider his options, herein after to be known as Mr. Out of the Closet, he decided that it would be best for all concerned to know the truth and that he was definitely Mr. Out of the Closet. Completely unsure of his emotional and social footing and because he was also afraid of being rejected by everyone, Mr. Out of the Closet asked me to be the bearer of gay tidings to the Princess Goddess, so to speak.

My response to his request required that I not tell him how much the Princess Goddess hated him. I thought that it was really unnecessary for him to know just how much the Princess Goddess hated him. Mr. Out of the Closet was intelligent and I thought emotionally astute enough to suspect that the Princess Goddess wasn't all that happy about their break-up, but he was completely unaware of just how angry and spiteful the Princess Goddess had become. Mr. Out of the Closet wasn't able to grasp that the Princess Goddess would go to her grave hating him. He was also unaware that all of the girls that had been their mutual friends, except for me, also hated his guts.

I made the phone call to La Princess Goddess.. I didn't want to have to speak to the goddess face to face because this was their business, but I had agreed to be the messenger for Mr. Out of the Closet's very personal message to the Princess Goddess about his sexual orientation.

The call began with the usual. The Princess Goddess shed a few tears that were immediately followed by a litany of "Who in the hell does he think he is?" and several other bulleted phrases that would have made a Marine blush.

I waited patiently for her anger to subside a bit. I changed the subject several times before I was able to engage her in conversation other than the dreaded break-up. Once she relaxed a bit I decided to give her the news: "Ah, Princess Goddess, Mr. In/Out of the Closet wanted you to know that he's now Mr. Out of the Closet." The gravity of the sudden silence that filled the space between us was truly profound. I had assumed that the Princess Goddess, once pricked, couldn't maintain silence for more than a few seconds. To my surprise her silence was total and complete and lasted for at least a full minute. Suddenly, the silence was pierced by her raucous laugh. She elicited peals of laughter that led to unrestrained yucks and snorts. The Princess Goddess finally stopped laughing long enough to state: "Oh, is that why he broke up with me. I feel so much better now; I mean some of my best friends are gay!" She paused again, but ever so briefly before continuing: "You know, I think I knew it all along. I just knew that he was gay!"

The Princess Goddess and I were roommates for our sophomore year and I was certain that the problems that I had experienced with my first roommates was just a fluke; a thing from the past. But after a few weeks I began to notice a familiar coolness from the Princess Goddess. That coolness felt exactly like what it had felt like with my other roommates. The Princess Goddess was suddenly emotionally distant and oddly uncommunicative.

Our dorm room was deathly silent most of the time all except for the scratch of clothing being removed from cardboard boxes or the creak of a piece of old furniture being moved to a new spot. The stillness was broken by a light tapping at the door and Mr. Out of the Closet stepped into our room looking a bit sheepish. The Princess Goddess ran towards him and wrapped her arms tightly around his neck while simultaneously pecking him on the check and said: "I'm so very glad to see you. Did you have a great summer? You have to make time for us to hang out, you know, just to talk?"

Like me, Mr. Out of the Closet was taken aback by her effusive enthusiasm and her suggestive physical response to him. This type of physical response was clearly missing from their relationship when they were a couple. Attempting to stay in and maintain the moment, Mr. Out of the Closet managed a weak smile while looking over the top of the Princess Goddess's head at me, his eyes pleading for help as he managed to choke out: "Oh, it was okay. And sure...we'll get together to talk once we're all settled in." He continued, in a kind of breathy, nervous manner like he was trying to read whether or not she was judging him: "How was your summer?" The Princess Goddess grabbed his hand and physically pulled him onto her bed. Mr. Out of the Closet almost lost his balance as her momentum and strength seemed to increase as the two neared her bed. She sat, reclined quickly beneath him on her bed and beamed up at him, heat radiating from her body: "Oh do sit, or lay? We have so much to talk about." I could see the panic rising behind his eyes so I decided that it would be best for me to intervene before Mr. Out of the Closet decided to bolt from the room.

I casually interrupted them with: "Hey, Mr. Out of the Closet, would you mind giving me a hand? I have a box in the basement that's a little too heavy for me to bring up the stairs." He let out an audible sigh of relief and replied, "Yeah, sure. I'd love to." As we left the room I could have sworn that the Princess Goddess hissed at my back in lieu of throwing something sharp and heavy at my retreating back. When I returned to the room it was empty, although not literally. I tried to start a friendly conversation with the Princess Goddess despite the winter chill that coated the walls even though her breath was filled with red hot fumes escaping from her flaring nostrils. The thing was that the Princess Goddess never said one word to me but I keyed in on a familiar scent in the air that was the unmistakable scent of an angry goddess. Maybe it was the smell of acrimony, a distinctive smell that all goddesses emit whenever betrayed or angered.

My relationship with the Princess Goddess all but dried up and disappeared that fall semester while Mr. Out of the Closet and the Princess Goddess found a way to become best friends. Mr. Out of the Closet spent most of the semester segueing in and out of a relationship with me. My situation devolved to the point where I didn't have a relationship with either person while those two seemed to thrive on making me and my boyfriend increasingly uncomfortable whenever we all managed to be in the same place at the same time. The situation became unbearable and I was faced with being a pariah once again.

The emotional sea change began subtly. I began to notice that I wasn't invited along for outings and parties hosted by or merely attended by the Princess Goddess even if hosted in our dorm room. Mr. Out of the Closet began to blossom in his new found friendship with the Princess Goddess and her entourage. My life became a flashback to the previous year and the Princess Goddess and her friends invaded my space and none of the people in her clique spoke to me. And it didn't take long for Mr. Out of the Closet to meld himself to the group and he quickly became infected with the group dynamic and stopped speaking to me.

At some point, the sisterhood of the Princess Goddess and Mr. Out of the Closet began to fray. Mr. Out of the Closet had always been a solitary person who needed his space that is time away from a group, especially a group that was comprised solely of coeds who giggled and made snide remarks about almost everyone. I was at the top of their list. Whenever I happened to cross their space, regardless of whether or not they were in my room, their voices would drop to all but a whisper or all conversation would cease. My departure from the dorm room was always punctuated by a host of snickers and the not so silent, audible whispers of the "in" crowd of the Princess Goddess. I instinctively knew that my only tactic against the group was to try to be neutral which was almost impossible in such a volatile situation. There is nothing more dangerous than being in a situation where a woman has been shamed or feels shamed and you are on the opposite side of her emotion; it is indeed a very dangerous place to be.

The problem: I sincerely liked both of the players. But in the end, both players couldn't help but to turn their energies and their misguided feelings against me. I became the focal point of their unvoiced dissatisfaction with each other. The situation between the Princess Goddess and I continued to decline and eventually disintegrated to the point that my living arrangement became untenable once again.

The Princess Goddess became a proficient marionette. The sense of betrayal and hatred that she once felt for Mr. Out of the Closet was transferred to me. One day after Winter Break I was confronted by the Princess Goddess and one of her fellow goddesses. As I entered the room, hot venom poured out towards me like molten hot steel. The Princess Goddess spat: "I have always been certain from the very beginning that Mr. Out of the Closet was in love with you even though he asked me to date him." I was shocked by this inaccurate revelation. She continued heatedly: "How dare you remain friends with him 'after' he broke up with me! My feelings and my concerns should have been more important to you than your friendship with him and your loyalty to me should certainly be far more important than being fair!" I was stunned by her honesty. I was speechless. No one had ever asked me for undying, unquestioning allegiance; not my mother, not my father nor my brother or sister and yet, here stood a petite, enraged, brunette demanding that I give her my unquestioning allegiance.

It had never occurred to the Princess Goddess that I was quite capable of making decisions about whom I spent time with without her approval or disapproval. The Princess Goddess left our room in a huff leaving behind that unmistakable pungent, acrid smell of disapproval. The Princess Goddess and her band of sycophants decided that I needed to be taught a lesson so that I would understand where my place was in the world. So the squeeze play against me began. Unfortunately, I realized that my mother had been correct when she had told me years earlier that someone could jump out of the frying pan and into the fire; and that was direction that my social life was heading at break neck speed.

The situation continued to erode. My birthday party occurred late in the second semester and was an absolute disaster. The Princess Goddess arrived in our dorm room and quickly assessed that the celebration was for me. She, almost on cue, fell dramatically apart while moaning about some vague personal problem. Needless to say the party broke up immediately and the Princess Goddess left with Mr. Out of the Closet who tried desperately to comfort her. The next birthday party that I attended was a party for a member of the Princess Goddess's clique, and it ended exactly as mine had. The Princess Goddess had far reaching powers. It became clear that no one deserved friendship or companionship unless the Princess Goddess deemed that the friendship was acceptable.

The school year ended with the Princess Goddess and one of her close confidents taking an assumed conciliatory stance towards me one afternoon; conciliatory on the surface while the two made it quite clear that they thought that I should seek professional, mental help.

The well placed stiletto heel of a scorned female generally cuts cleanly across the lives of men and women. Few men are able to understand or withstand the assault of a scorned woman but the assault of a full-fledged goddess is something to behold and nothing that anyone should ever have to endure. But for most women who were raised by other women and were taught to interact with and trust other women, the enigma of the goddess complex is at once a positive social construct as well as a negative social bane.

Most little girls learned to share their secrets with other little girls and nothing is better than the trusting friendship that can develop between innocent little girls. The dream of real friendship becomes tainted by jealousy and insecurity and the thought of being friendless is a concept that many young girls just can't accept. Young goddesses learn how to be mean from the mean women in their lives. The need to 'belong' for most women is so intense that many women literally trade their self-worth and values just to be included in. Friendship in these circumstances is turned into a sick symbiotic relationship that functions only to please the head goddess. Many women learned how to play power games way back in middle school where other girls learn to kowtow to the demands of the mean girls in the popular group.

It would seem that it would be a blessing for men and non-goddess women to refrain from intimate contact with goddess types because of the numerous broken bodies and souls that goddesses leave behind in their wake. But the sad reality is, all goddesses have a type of magnetism that attracts and holds the attention of an audience that needs to be in close contact with, and at times, abused by someone in the goddess class. As long as there are people who prefer to take orders rather than to take the initiative and the responsibility to be the captain of their own ship, then there will be people, goddesses, who will gladly step-up to orchestrate a world that makes them happy and secure even though they are causing others untold pain. Goddesses are mean and self-motivated women that thrive on other people's discomfort. A sad fact of life is that goddesses will continue to flourish at the expense of the rest of us.

Unasked For Advice
Chapter 3

What is the most annoying thing about women to men? Most men would respond: "That unending flow of unasked for advice." It is true that most women offer unasked for advice to everyone but goddesses go well beyond just offering unasked for advice to family, friends and foes. We have all been plagued by this accepted female phenomenon without realizing that the people most guilty of offering a lot of unasked for advice are goddesses. Most of us are compelled to endure that endless flow of advice from the goddesses in our lives. If unasked for advice from a goddess falls on deaf ears, then the receiver of that advice is in grave danger of receiving even more unasked for advice.

The question becomes: how does someone differentiate between harmless unasked for advice and deleterious unasked for advice from a goddess? The task is difficult to master because generally, unasked for advice typically falls on the ears of children and husbands and the only thing that kids and hubbies hear is: "blah, blah, blah." Goddesses on the other hand offer do more than offer advice. Goddesses insist that other people to follow their advice and act without questioning. Hence, Goddesses find it very easy and acceptable to offer unasked for advice to mere acquaintances or even total strangers.

For those who suffer from the goddess complex, it just never occurs to them that the world is full of talented people with their own ideas about how to solve life's problems. For the goddess, it never occurs to them that there could be other ways, maybe great other ways, to successfully complete a task or to solve a problem.

The next time that you go out to the mall or to a restaurant, take the time to look at the people around you. You will find it very easy to determine if it is a woman or a goddess proffering unasked for advice. If the man sitting with the woman at the restaurant is idly reading a newspaper, it is a safe guess that the woman talking isn't a goddess. If you watch most couples long enough you'll be able to determine the exact moment when a man's attention begins to drift from the conversation. The signs of his mental drift are unmistakable. There is a distinct softening of his facial features, his eyes are engaged somewhere far beyond his wife's person and his eyes belie the obvious disconnect that he is somewhere faraway. Just where he is at the moment is unclear but that is okay because the man is at peace.

I began to recognize that look on my father's face as my mother's voice droned on and on about things that didn't hold interest for either of us. My mother was notorious for holding court and when she spoke, in her mind, the rest of the world had to come to a complete stop and listen. My father was the most patient man that I have known and upon reflection, he had to be just to survive all those years living with my mother. If it isn't clear, my mother was a goddess. And my father learned, like many other men who are married to goddesses, how to 'appear" interested in every word that falls from his goddess's perfect lips. A lot of these men 'appear' to be listening intently when in fact he's really just reading his daily newspaper. Most of whatever the goddess is saying to her man is lost somewhere in the ether that exists between men and women.

The following is a live action drama that happens somewhere a zillion times a day between a normal woman and a normal male. There is an unspoken, uncharted dance that occurs between the listener (male) and the purveyor of information (female) where someone might notice the exact moment in a conversation when the woman asks the man a question that requires a response from him. Of course the male is consumed by his interest in the daily newspaper or a brief fantasy to actually notice a change in the rhythm or tone of his wife's voice. The unschooled male ear misses the unmistakable pause in her conversation that demands a response from him and when her cold silence descends upon the poor male, he is shocked back into consciousness and invariably responds inappropriately to her query with an inappropriate "huh!" The male realizes much too late that he has missed that all important cue and will pay for his inattentiveness.

The more clever males are quick to rebound in such circumstances. The smart ones manage to return a conversational volley that momentarily confuses the female: "Oh honey, I'm sorry, that passing car drowned out what you were saying." Or he might say, "You know I missed the first few words that you said. Hon, would you repeat it for me?" If this phrase doesn't turn her bruised feelings away from anger, he then begins to work a little bit harder by trying to gain her sympathy: "Honey, you know my hearing's shot! The war and all those jets taking off and landing... blah, blah, and blah. So ah, Hon, what was that you were saying?" Every woman who lives with a man has heard the "poor hearing excuse" at least once. But most women have experienced their hearing impaired mates being able to hear in less than perfect situations. It's amazing what a hearing impaired male can hear either outside in the yard with the lawn mower going full blast or if he's in the shower with the water turned to full capacity. This hearing impaired male manages to overhear everything said in a conversation that concerns or is about him without missing a single syllable. Many men miraculously regain the ability to hear a pin drop or a twig snap in the woods if the conversation is remotely about them. In other words, most men have selective hearing. So, it is relatively safe to say that most men are either born with or develop selective hearing by the time they experience that surge of testosterone.

The following will illustrate the difference between normal female advice and goddess unasked for advice. Normal females offer advice about what to eat for breakfast or what color tie her husband should wear with a certain suit or shirt. Goddesses on the other hand offer unasked for advice about issues that are highly personal.

My youngest daughter is actually the spawn of her father and I but like most women I refer to our children as 'my children' as if I conceived them all by myself. Anyway, the youngest of our three children began to play soccer, reluctantly, when she was twelve. Being the baby, I allowed her to avoid joining team sports until twelve unlike her brother and sister who started playing team sports at six. My youngest daughter's desire to play soccer like her siblings and my need for penance to absolve me from the sin of being an out-of-control soccer mom, I also volunteered to join the board and to schedule referees for games for our entire region. I ended up working closely with the region's soccer commissioner.

The board was comprised mostly of males and the commissioner's wife was not a member of the board, nor was she involved with the business of the soccer club unless she attended her daughter's games. Over the months and years, I had contact with the commissioner's wife simply because I made a habit of calling the wives of referee's to staff the games. Husbands who were referees would routinely ask me to talk directly with their wives about their weekend schedules and when she felt he could ref a game or two. Making contact with the wives ensured that my games always had adequate referee coverage.

As the years passed, I had brief contact with the commissioner's wife. The commissioner's wife was a goddess and I had vowed many years before to refrain from dealing with goddesses. Since our daughters played on the same soccer team that was coached by her husband it was literally impossible for me not to run into Mrs. Commissioner. Mrs. Commissioner was in her mid-forties, didn't meet trophy wife standards and was referred to by her husband as 'the warden.' I believe that the commissioner knew his wife better than I did therefore she will be named the Warden Goddess.

The Warden Goddess was about 5'5". She had brunette hair and was of medium build. On the whole, there was absolutely nothing physically spectacular about the Warden Goddess. Although she wasn't a trophy wife she was a social hub in our community because of her stellar volunteer efforts. The commissioner was a ruddy-faced, curly haired Irish looking man who by day was a bond trader and spent the rest of his time as a soccer coach and top dog of our soccer organization. In other words, the man spent a lot of time away from home. Rising to the level and stature of commissioner demonstrated that he had spent many years on the board and volunteered many hours to this soccer organization. And the coolest thing about the commissioner: he sincerely enjoyed his job as commissioner. He made my job easy because he was so easy to work with. But then life, as most of us live it, arises and unforeseen problems tumble out.

It was a typical Saturday evening during soccer season. All of the games had been completed hours earlier and my family and I had just finished dinner. We were settled down to watch a movie. The phone rang. I answered the intruding call a bit brusquely. "Hello." To my surprise, it was the Warden Goddess.

I had spoken to the Warden Goddess on a few occasions but those occasions always happened because I needed to have information conveyed to the commissioner. Whenever I called her home to leave a message, the Warden Goddess always made it clear that she couldn't talk long because she was in a hurry to go somewhere to do something that was always more important than anything I had to say. The call from the Warden Goddess should have been a clue to me that something was wrong with this picture. My second clue should have been that Warden Goddess wasn't in a rush to get off the telephone with me.

The conversation began innocently enough, that is, innocent if you're the village idiot and are unaware of the fact that the villagers decided to burn Frankenstein. A practicing goddess, the Warden Goddess began the conversation innocently: "I hope that I'm not intruding?" This is an example of typical goddess speak. The Warden Goddess had never been concerned with me, my feelings or my time. She assumed that I was at her beck and call because she was married to the commissioner. On guard I responded: "Oh, no! We just finished dinner. How can I help you?" There was a brief silence as the Warden Goddess collected her thoughts. She began tentatively: "Ah…do you mind if I ask you something personal?" Now, this type of question is always framed in classic goddess speak. In response to her apparent softball question, the hairs on the back of my neck stood-up and I silently thought: here we go again but I responded with: "No, of course not. What would you like to know?" I closed my eyes in expectation as the Warden Goddess began to weave her web. "Okay, since you don't mind…I was wondering, who is that man that's always with you at the soccer games?" Unfortunately, I relaxed once I heard her generic questions. My reply was relaxed: "He's my husband." The Warden Goddess sucked in an audible breath, a bit exasperated: "No, I mean that man who's always with you?" My signals were screaming out of control but I managed to respond to her calmly: "He's my husband. We've been married for thirty plus years. We married when I was seventeen." Not to be silenced on the issue the Warden Goddess plunged on: "Were you married before? Was he married before?" I was having difficulty trying to understand why any of this had any relevance and why she was interested in me and my marital status at all.

I attempted to break the tension that I was feeling by giving the goddess a brief overview of my married life. I informed her that we had three children and that my youngest was my twentieth wedding anniversary gift. Apparently the Warden Goddess wasn't blessed with higher level critical math skills because she then asked: "Why is he so close to Chloe? (Chloe is our youngest) I always see them together at games." In reply there was only one way to respond: "He's her father." But the Warden Goddess continued to ask questions that just didn't make sense to me, that is if she had been listening: "I just don't understand why Chloe is so close to him. If I were you I'd spend more time trying to find out why they're so comfortable with one another." On that note I decided that the woman was crazy. But of course she wasn't crazy. This was just the way that this goddess chose to tell me that she objected to my relationship with my husband and the father of my children. This is an example of classic goddess speak. And if I had been a different sort of person, I might have taken her criticism to heart and my marriage might have begun to unravel because of her criticism. It would be nice to have said that this was the last time that I spoke to the Warden Goddess; sadly, it wasn't.

Weeks passed and the soccer season ended but a brand new season was on the horizon. I stayed in my position as the Referee Scheduler for a total of three years. The job had always been time consuming and onerous but I always managed to take satisfaction in the fact that the games were always staffed with qualified referees. Towards the end of my tenure to the commissioner and the board, the Warden Goddess decided that it was her duty to verbally chastise me about how she felt that I should handle my duties as ref scheduler.

As usual, I was making calls to referees and/or their spouses, typically on Wednesday afternoons and the task always resulted in the afternoon turning into evening. As a general rule, I avoided calling the commissioner to pinch hit as a referee because his plate was already overflowing. But on occasion, I had no choice but to call the commissioner and request his help. This particular Wednesday was one of those rare occasions; the number of people that had the time to ref games on the upcoming weekend wasn't sufficient. So, I began to beat the bushes. The first calls went out to other board members who enjoyed lesser status than the big kahuna, the commissioner. As I plowed my way through the list, I began to realize that I was going to have to call the commissioner.

The commissioner had always been a nice, helpful and dedicated man. Whatever I had asked of him in the past, he had always managed to give me what I needed. I am certain that the commissioner was completely aware that I never called to ask him to ref a game unless it was absolutely necessary.

Even though I owned and operated my own business, I had always managed to schedule refs to cover the games. The upcoming weekend was also a holiday weekend and many families were leaving town. It was a Thursday morning and I had to call the Warden Goddess to ask her to have the commissioner to call me later in the day.

Here begins another lesson in classic goddess speak.. These are the types of encounters that almost every woman who is not a goddess instinctively knows should be avoided at all costs. It is important to note that I had not spoken to the Warden Goddess since her inquiries about my husband and his relationship with our daughter. Before dialing the number I gave myself a quick pep talk: "Self, you can handle this woman. Remember this is about the three hundred children who play soccer every weekend. This is not about the Warden Goddess. So, suck it up and make the call."

The moment that the woman recognized my voice on the other end of the line she began with: "oh, sorry. I have to leave. I have workers in my home at the moment and I need to run and pick up some refreshments for them." I responded with: "Oh, I'm so sorry. I didn't know." Of course I didn't know that she had workmen in her home. She and I never had a conversation that lasted more than five minutes except on the evening when she decided that she had to just ask "something personal." "Again, I apologize for intruding on your busy schedule Mrs. Warden Goddess but could you have Mr. Commissioner give me a call this evening?" She replied sharply: "Why? What do you want?" Her stinging reply found its mark and I felt like the dear goddess had hit me. I managed to inhale and continued on: "I need to speak to him about the games this weekend. I hoped that he could ref a game or two?" She responded with silence. She was silent for so long that I almost thought that we had been disconnected. Finally she responded. Her tone and manner shifted and she made me feel like she was either my boss or my mother. Of course she was neither.

Gloves clearly off, she spat at me: "Exactly why do you wait so late in the week to schedule games?" Her response caught me off guard and as a volunteer I have never had anyone criticize how or when I choose to fulfill my obligations to the organization. Perturbed and insulted I snapped back: "Since when is it your job to monitor when I schedule refs?" She responded with silence again. I decided that her tone and silence weren't enough to make me feel guilty about her criticism and I was definitely not going to change my behavior. Her response baffled me. Her response clearly indicated that one of us was an idiot and I was convinced that it surely wasn't me. "In case you've forgotten, I'm the commissioner's wife. You will answer to me just as you would answer to him." At this point the lady began to sound as if I were on her payroll. "Now, why are you making calls so late in the week to schedule games? You should schedule games during the weekend!"

Now, let's examine the Warden Goddess's assumptions. First of all, the goddess assumed that my social standing was beneath hers therefore she also assumed my value as a human being was less. Note: All goddesses believe that they are better than other people and therefore have rights and privileges that other people aren't people shouldn't enjoy. Her second assumption was that because her husband was the commissioner and because she was married to him that she too had been anointed with his inherent power. To my knowledge the Warden Goddess had never attended a board meeting nor had she ever coached a soccer game much less refereed a game. But in her goddess mind she perceived herself to be "in charge" and expected me to dance to her tune.

The call ended badly. I knew that I was going to resign my position at the end of the season because three years is a long to time schedule referees for AYSO soccer games. I actually responded to the women with distinct, quiet steel: "If you must know, I work. I schedule games when it fits into my schedule not when it suits you. Have your husband call me this evening and I'll ask him if he'd like me to resign now because I'm certain that you could so much better." To sum it up, I finished the season and the Warden Goddess's husband along with the rest of the board complimented me for the service I had performed for the organization for three years. The commissioner made it quite clear in his speech that I would be hard to replace. So if you're keeping score the stats now are: – Goddesses 1 - Regular Chicks 1.

But of course, I wasn't blessed and the Warden Goddess wasn't the last goddess to offer me unasked for advice. Regular women are considered by goddesses to be beneath their class both socially and economically. Many goddesses don't need to pursue a rewarding career although many goddesses have attended some of the finest universities that America has to offer. Many goddesses attended these fine, prestigious universities with the sole intent of bagging Mr. Right.

Almost all normal women have received unwanted advice from goddesses. Goddesses are all too happy to respond to other women with problems by offering platitudes and palliates meant to shift attention back to themselves. If a woman is contemplating divorce because her husband is an obvious cheater, or an abuser, you can bet that the goddess will offer profound insight into the situation and say: "But, what about the children?" If a woman was contemplating to either marry or remarry the man of her dreams the goddess would certainly say: "You know… you really shouldn't marry him…he's no good for you!" Each statement is delivered with ease by the goddess as she hungrily eyes the man of another woman's dreams. Occasionally, a goddess will deign to actually visit you at your home. During the visit the goddess will find something that doesn't suit her taste or liking which then leads to her being critical about the décor of the house, choice of cooking pans, the cleanliness of the home and/or children, ad infinitum until this advice stretches to include any and all things that really shouldn't anyone.

All women, at one time or another has had a well-meaning friend or a stranger walk-up and offer unasked for advice to them on how to discipline an inconsolable child in the grocery store or how to match colors your basic personality. For most women, it is not unthinkable that a relative stranger, almost always female, would enter their personal comfort zone and to tell them that they should have done something, differently. The advice that normally comes from a regular woman is benign whereas the advice given by a goddess is typically inappropriate and often mean in content. Let's say that you're employed full-time in a high profile profession. A regular woman might suggest that you are overworked woman and should think seriously about hiring outside help do household chores and maybe even cook for their family. A goddess, on the other hand could not stop herself from lecturing the working mom about how she is cheating her children and her husband because she should be at home taking care of her kids and husband.

To decimate another not so big secret: women really do dress to impress other women. Although women want to be attractive to men, women really dress to keep other women from forming negative assumptions about them based on their style of dress, their social status or their economic stability. Many modern males have made it very clear that most men don't really care what a woman is wearing, just as long as she is attractive to him. So, that multi-billion dollar fashion industry is not based on what pleases men but it is based on what women think and like. Almost all women believe that women are born with an innate fashion sense but goddesses are always, ALWAYS ready to offer 'helpful' advice about someone's personal style and what that style should look like even if the unasked for advice from the goddess doesn't appeals to their sense of style. Ah, but wait! Of course the never ending unasked for advice from the goddesses doesn't end with a course in fashion: the unasked for fashion advice somehow morphs into the minutiae of how you live your life and also encompasses the lives of their friends as well.

It's obvious that all this unbidden, unasked for advice from the goddess class has fallen on my somewhat deaf ears. Over the years I have received so much unbidden, unasked for advice from goddesses that I've actually built up a tolerance for how to avoid unasked for advice. Like men sitting at the breakfast table reading their newspapers, I will my mind not to listen. I've learned how and when to smile at the right times throwing in a nod or two of my head to imply interest. In my youth I became angry with goddesses who thought that they knew more about my life and needs than I did.

The goddess gene requires goddesses to disseminate unasked for advice to others that isn't needed and is oftentimes unwanted. A lot of unasked for advice from goddesses is about how a regular woman can gain entrance into their closed society or how to make a man do what she wants him to do. Truthfully, in the mind of the goddess, she considers herself to be the unquestioned authority on almost everything. If her advice is discarded without deep contemplation or an attempt to follow her unasked for advice, the goddess typically responds with a haughty, arrogant attitude that devolves into an unreasonable discourse between a rationale woman and a petulant goddess.

Women, who tend to give friendly advice, asked for or not, are all around us. Women we work with, women we attend church with, women we meet in passing or in beauty salons, grocery stores, and of course the PTA, Little League, Softball, or AYSO. The world is filled with women who have volumes of advice to share with others and the foregoing list hasn't taken into account the women that we can't get away from, meaning our beloved mothers, sisters, or other female relatives and friends.

Most people recognize that the PTA is a wonderful organization. The rank and file positions within the PTA are typically filled by non-working mothers who make sure that the teachers and students are supported in their educational needs and a few extra curricula goals that are not met by state or local funding. But then there is another group of women who typically become President, Vice President, Secretary or Treasurer of the local school PTA. These positions are generally filled by ladies who socialize with one another outside of school functions and these women typically pass their idle time together at the local spa or hair salon. Like corporate America, the local chapters of every organization that function primarily because of female volunteers manages to physically resemble one another simply because the membership of these organizations are filled with people that live, think, and worship in much the same way.

Over the years, I have joined the PTA but I never been anything more than a card carrying member. Oh sure, I have volunteered and worked in various classrooms to keep my ear close to what was happening in my children's school lives and what specifically was or wasn't happening for them academically. My idea about volunteering has always been a bit like allowing my home to be the central meeting place for my kids and their friends after school and on the weekends; I considered my so-called largess a necessity that allowed me to gain a glimpse inside my children's world and their lives that I might not have otherwise been allowed to observe. To my thinking, this vantage point has been a valuable tool that allowed me to see the type of kids that my children hung-out with and whether or not my kids were acquiring a solid education. Over the years, because I supplied food and a kind of relaxed freedom in my home, many of my children's friends thought that I was the 'coolest' when in fact I was simply being a master detective.

Anyway, as fate would have it, some of the ladies who populate the ranks of the PTA are also goddesses. Many PTA goddess moms are simply grown-up mean girls. Somehow, mysteriously, the goddesses who live within a certain geographic location are able to assemble in one organization to give the rest of us grief. The goddesses always manage to conduct awards ceremonies designed principally to honor themselves. I have been invited to these celebrations over the years by hard-working, well-meaning teachers because of the hours that I have volunteered in their classrooms. Many of these teachers don't normally attend these functions and have no idea that these celebrations have very little to do with the students or the needs of the school.

During the final "ceremony" of the PTA year, the goddesses in charge plan an evening filled with their beguiling personal stories. Each honoree steps up to the microphone and shares her story of how she met and married her successful husband or about whatever prestigious university she attended and what sorority she pledged and was accepted by. All of this unimportant information being regurgitated in front of a weary audience at the end of a long workday simply bordered on cruelty. After the passage of the first tortuous hour every goddess honoree is gushing with pride as the recitations of their life stories continues, unabated while audience members shift uncomfortably in their chairs while attempting to stave off sleep. You see, when goddesses aren't giving unasked for advice they are staging activities to honor themselves.

On the night of celebration, the very air in the auditorium was giddy with excitement and anticipation, that is, if you were a goddess and being honored for something. The goddesses have hoodwinked their husbands into attending this self aggrandizement activity regardless of the fact the husband had worked ten or twelve hours or may have just returned from an exhaustive business trip. Most husbands looked tired, drawn and uncomfortable in their suits and their starched, shirts and slightly unloosened ties. Each man was flawlessly dressed in that de rigueur suit that all professional, executive males don and not one man had a clue about how to inform their goddess wives that they needed to go home for some much needed rest.

Everyone in the audience sat attentively and listened to the speeches that had little to do with the school, the students or what it was that the honorees had accomplished to receive their distinctive awards. The point is; well-meaning people were needlessly subjected to several hours of unasked for information that should have been called the Goddess Prime Time Show.

The goddess has hubris running through her veins because they find it quite acceptable to squander other people's time. Most of the goddesses who man the governing positions within the PTA almost always have an established relationship with all other goddesses in the organization. Goddesses have a knack for creating groups that are exclusive and their organizations often manage to exclude others who have valuable skills that might enhance the organization. Being principally self-centered, goddesses thrive on mutual adoration.

But over the years, women have begun to have influence over more than PTA activities in the schools. Just look at some of the ways that our lives have been irreparably changed in the last twenty-five years because of goddesses. In the early 1990's "zero-tolerance" was adopted as a policy in many schools. Too be sure, the phalanx of support was headed by goddesses. Many of these changes began in our schools and have filtered into the rest of society because of goddesses. Although many embraced zero-tolerance as an ideology many were also women who were prone to overreacting to situations. This vanguard of women also worked tirelessly on projects that aimed to change or to protect children from threat or danger became buoyed by the idea that zero-tolerance would make schools safer.

Zero tolerance as a philosophy began in schools to discourage drug use and violence against other students. What has resulted in schools since "zero tolerance" was adopted is that asthma inhalers have become a listed, forbidden drug and plastic butter knives have become lethal weapons. Once upon a time, parents, teachers and school administrators worked together to ensure that all students were safe while at school. Zero tolerance as a concept would have been shunned as a ludicrous idea for any educator to even contemplate.

The issues that confront teachers and school administrators could probably fill the pages of another book and most of those issues have nothing to do with properly educating a population of young people to become contributing members of society. Much of what teachers and administrators have to deal with today in schools are because of parents who believe that they and their children are privileged in ways that others are not. Most modern-day parents don't discipline their children and don't want others to do so either. We live in a society where misbehaving has become expected and protected. To gain media attention all anyone has to do is do commit some highly anti-social act.

At some point, long before 9/11, Americans decided that their personal safety was more important than rational thought. The American public has been duped into believing that passage of tougher laws will ensure greater safety. The reality is that the sacrifice of fundamental freedoms has actually made us more vulnerable. Perceived, unexplained fear is almost largely a feminine trait that is emotionally passed to the men in their lives. Many of the fears that coalesce in women and cause them to act proactively are at times based on a sense of physical vulnerability and a general sense of powerlessness. Younger women have fought their fears about physical vulnerability and many no longer accept or feel powerless.

While I was still a full-time, working mom, I used to drive my daughter to school. The school was located across town about twenty-minutes away by freeway. After the drop-off I would make a stop by the Rose Bowl for a morning stroll (approximately 3.2 miles). The morning crowd at the Rose Bowl is typically comprised of men, women, young athletes and a brash young group of executives made up of men and women. Many of the people who walk around the Rose Bowl in the morning/evenings live in the surrounding neighborhoods, but others, like me, stop while passing through the area en route to somewhere else. Many of these people are professional women who have time to exercise before they have to report to the office. The rest are typically goddesses who have the leisure of being stay-at-home moms manning strollers with either sleeping or fidgeting babies. Body obsessed, the goddess decides to get back into shape by taking a morning walk with friends before turning the baby over to the nanny.

One morning during my trek, I managed to end up behind two young women who were both probably in their early to mid-twenties. One of the young ladies was complaining because her husband had received a new credit card from a low-end department store while that same low-end department store had declined to issue her a separate credit card in her name. As an ex-banker I decided to interrupt the two to provide them with some information from a credit grantor's point of view, and what steps the young lady should take to initiate and solve her current credit dilemma. Well, to assume that my desire to impart information was a wrong move should have been an elementary assumption because I soon found out that I had committed a major faux pas. I attempted to dispense unasked for advice to a goddess.

Ms Friend Goddess was a young woman with auburn hair; about 5'8" tall, a slender 115 lbs. dressed in stylish exercise togs. Ms. Credit Spurned Goddess was a bit shorter saddled with problem thighs. At the sound of my voice, the Credit Spurned Goddess immediately stopped in her tracks and whirled about in response to my uttered pearls of wisdom that obviously fell on and offended her delicate ears. The Spurned Credit Goddess appeared to blow-up, physically, as in expand, dramatically. I felt like I was in one of those nature shows wherein a predator comes face to face with its prey. The goddess's size literally began to expand and grow before my eyes. She appeared to be much taller and her body seemed to ripple with muscles while the color rose in her creamy, perfect white cheeks. Puffing with anger and not exertion, she regarded me as if I were an alien from a far and distant planet. In a way, her observation was completely correct because I had deigned to offer her unbidden, unasked for advice advice. It was clear from the look on her face that if she could have, she would have turned me into a pillar of stone, a likely punishment for someone who had so inappropriately crossed her boundaries.

My offense, rather my crime, was that I intruded into her world, without an invitation. I might have been Moses with that rumored third tablet tucked securely under his robed arm, ready to enlighten with those hidden secrets and rituals that would have ensured that the goddess would never have to face unhappiness or turned-down credit again. Obviously I wasn't Moses and it was just as obvious that Ms. Credit Spurned Goddess wasn't going to heed any advice from me. Besides, the information that I offered her was free and everyone knows that anything given freely isn't valuable, right?

Ms. Credit Spurned Goddess curled her perfect lips into a grimace and hissed at me: "Mind your own damn business and stay out of mine." I tried to brush my embarrassment aside: "Sorry to have intruded (first mistake, never admit wrong doing to a goddess) but I'm a banker and I approve credit and make loans everyday..." Ms. Credit Spurned Goddess's annoyance peaked as she interrupted me with "I don't care who or what you are! Get away from me!" The goddess's eyes flashed a smoldering heat warning that portended to be quite lethal. It was clear that a major storm was about to strike if I persisted as her tone devolved into an insult.

Another distasteful rub with the goddess class is that they are always the 'all knowing ones' while everyone else, whether a mother, a husband or a child never has the right to disagree with them and please God, never, ever correct a goddess. That sad fact is that so many goddesses are so woefully uninformed about anything they're not interested in; hence many goddesses make crude and very often cruel observations about other people and events that they consider to be valueless.

All of this free-flowing helpful and unasked for advice from the ranks of goddesses is generally not helpful and it is never free. Generally, the goddess dispensing unasked for advice has some ulterior motive for taking the time to offer this "free," unasked for advice to a non-goddess. Goddesses are highly motivated and many have twisted reasons for being involved with people they consider their 'lessers.'

So, beware the goddess who is offering unasked for advice.

Sisterhood - The Great Lie
Chapter 4

The last three decades of the 20th century have been dominated by women's issues, at least in the United States. Although hordes of women have lobbied and demonstrated for their rights, the fact remains that many young women still desire to live lives engaged in traditional relationships. Most unattached women prefer to have the same things that their mothers or grandmothers had according to popular female talk shows like Oprah; a husband, a home filled with growing and happy children and for some, a career. Over the past thirty years women have made great strides in their quest to attain equality in the workplace and those changes made in the workplace have also affected the home front as well. Yet the battle for complete equality and autonomy has not yielded equal pay for equal work for women in the same professions as men. Although many feminists continue to work tirelessly to change workplace inequalities for women the waters have been muddied for all women by feminist goddesses.

For the working goddess, truth for them is based solely on what they want and goddesses typically demand preferential treatment under the guise of seeking full autonomy. This bait and switch routine leads to my fourth "hate," that is, women who are in reality seeking preferential treatment rather than full equality for all women and all people in general. The workplace goddesses are only motivated by their quest for economic equality in a man's and consequently not interested in the plight of real hard-working, dedicated women who clearly aren't goddesses and would never be referred to as "those women." Often times, 'those women' tend to be at the top of their game, and yet these privileged women continue to moan about how they aren't respected or treated fairly by men and society at large. And to make matters even worse, few of these goddesses are ever inclined or motivated to reach down and help other women to successfully climb the corporate ladder.

Without a doubt, America is one of the most litigious societies on the face of the earth. Under the flag of the feminist movement, women, in their not so quiet quest for equality, have attempted to not only change how women are treated in the workplace but also how women should be regarded in the world. It goes without saying that changes were sorely needed in our society to ensure that women and minorities received fair treatment in the workplace because each of these groups has experienced unfair treatment in the workplace and the courts for decades. Part of the mistreatment that these two groups have experienced lies in the fact that society has always judged women and minorities as second class despite the implied inclusion of these groups in the Bill of Rights. Although women experience greater freedoms and workplace inclusion as never before, women, like minorities, still haven't achieved full economic equality in modern American society.

Many women in the United States begin their work careers very soon after they graduate from high school. Like a lot of other women, I began to work when I was eighteen years old. Like so many other women I was eager to learn and perform my duties skillfully. In the process of becoming skillful, my zeal and attention to detail was recognized by my superiors and I, like tens of thousands of other women, landed in positions where one of my primary duties was to train men how to do the job. Back in the day, meaning the late sixties through the mid-eighties, every man that I had ever trained earned significantly more money than I, even during their training period. To add insult to injury, within a very short time frame, my 'trainee' would be promoted and become the new department manager while I continued to train a constant flow of college grads that largely turned out to be 'ninety day wonders.'

Becoming a supervisor is a somewhat easy task for a lot of women to accomplish. On the other hand, for those very same dedicated and hard-working women it is very difficult to become a senior manager and then move into the executive ranks of vice president and beyond. 1967 was the year that I began to work and at that time it was almost impossible for women to gain promotions that would eventually lead to upper management in banking or most other fields for that matter. There were few, if any, female branch bank managers in 1967. Not even in the liberal state of California.

The working reality for many women from the late 1960's until today is the same: the majority of males earn more money than their female counterparts performing the exact same job. Until women are equally compensated for doing the exact same job as men the notion of equality becomes more like a blighted landscape than a truth for working women who are underpaid to perform the same duties as their male counterparts for lesser compensation. This visible and active acceptance of inequality between men and women in the workplace continues to fuel an unspoken, yet vibrant feud between the sexes.

The reality that afflicts both men and women and how well they relate to one another at home and in the workplace is all too often a landscape filled with invisible landmines for both groups. I suspect that the real wars between men and women, that is, those unspoken wars, will always be waged about issues that have nothing to do with gender equality. Both men and women continue to lose something of great value in these pointed, silent wars and neither gender will ever be declared the winner.

This section of the book is not about the feminists and the war that they have waged for equality in the workplace but it is about the goddesses who seriously believe that they should receive special treatment; especially in the workplace.

In the past, goddesses were expected to run a proper home and ensure that the children were properly raised. The boys born into these upper echelon families were supposed to grow-up and pursue a successful career like their father's and the girls in the family were supposed to grow-up and be beautiful, charming and smart enough to attract a husband who was economically successful and had a direct access to power.

The new Affirmative Action movement ushered into the American workplace a new breed of goddess who not only expected equal pay, benefits and perks for their efforts in the workplace but many of these well-heeled goddesses also sought to change the emotional dynamic between men and women. Many men find it difficult to relate to women in the same way that they relate to other men. The workplace movement resulted in feminists talking points that also included on how male employees should act around female employees. Today, it is near next to impossible for a male employee to compliment a female employee on her choice of attire, hairstyle, or to say that he appreciates her particular brand of attractiveness or even her choice of perfume without cracking the door to a harassment lawsuit or, at the very least, a write-up for conduct that could lead to termination.

During the years that I was a banker, both as a line employee and as a manager, I managed to walk away from private industry with one clear observation: people are a lot like rabbits. Part of my early work life was spent in a bank data processing department. Working in the data processing center was an eye opener in that there were more sexual liaisons occurring during lunch on the rooftop parking lot than in most college dorm rooms. Maybe the proliferation of sexual liaisons at the data center was a consequence of people working the swing shift or possibly because the bank employed large numbers of sexually frustrated and unsatisfied men and women. Maybe having to work in such close proximity to one another, night after night, made the late lunch hour on the roof in closed, hot, steamy cars so popular for late night sexual frenzy?

Anyway, being eighteen and truly innocent I can truthfully state that no man or woman ever approached me with lust or desire in their eyes. Or, maybe I was just too innocent and stupid to be able to recognize lust. But I am certain of one thing: everyone who worked on this shift thought that I was a complete baby despite the fact that I had been married for over a year. My next place of employment was filled with the stuff of sexual harassment lawsuit dreams. The time for sexual harassment lawsuits was twenty years in the future and not something anyone thought about in the late 1960's. The time frame occurred a few years before the "burn the bra" era coupled with other feminist sentiments while many young people in the nation were emotionally eclipsed by the love, peace, and happiness mantra of the day.

I once worked for a now defunct bank in the mythical but very real city of Beverly Hills, California. My college education was still in progress therefore I had no choice but to work the swing shift because

I was a full-time student. My boss at the time was a gregarious, good-looking, blue—eyed good ole boy from Arizona. He was also quite proud to admit that he was a redneck and would never consider having sex with any woman who wasn't white.

The fashion code back in the day was essentially ultra short mini-skirts and dresses that barely covered the curve of a well formed buttock and see-through blouses. The first six months I worked at the facility my blue-eyed boss made sure that I had a healthy dose of daily off-color jokes. I was once again the youngest person in the facility; therefore I was also the target of most of the sex jokes because I was the new fair game in the department. My boss and the other guys in the computer room teased me unmercifully; but the burden of my daily ribbing fell onto the shoulders of my good natured, good-looking boss. At least once a week, my boss, with high mischief dancing behind those blue eyes, would invite me into his office to hear his rendition of some new off-color joke that always ended with him inquiring if I had any interest in meeting his one-eared elephant. The gist of his one-eared elephant caper, if you've never been exposed to the joke before, is played out when a guy pulls out one of his front pants pockets and begins to unzip his fly. I'm certain that you can imagine the rest of the picture although I never actually saw the completion of the joke. Being too young to understand that all I had to do was to call his bluff and to stand there and wait for him to unmask the monster, an action that would have stopped his daily harassment. Instead, the only thing I could think to do was to make a fast retreat out of his office and hope against all hope that he would decide to never try to embarrass me again.

I spent eons, (at least in my mind), being embarrassed by him and this trick and for a while I was pleased that I had always made it out of his office before his pants were halfway unzipped. My fast departure from his office was always followed by the rich tones of his deep, masculine laugh. Even though I was the butt of this joke on multiple occasions I never felt sexually harassed. I knew that it was a joke and that he meant me no harm.

Of course this was all in fun in a fast paced, tension filled environment and everyone needed something to break the tension that built up as our nightly deadlines neared. The funny thing was that I was completely aware that my boss was just a jokester and that he had no interest in me sexually at all. I was just the perfect target for his very juvenile jokes. At the time I was very quiet and shy but my shyness never prevented me from vowing that one day I'd pay him back for making me the butt of his jokes. My boss of course laughed off what he considered to be my idle threats as he continued to tell me even more salacious jokes. As an only child, I learned early on that sometimes the only weapon that the powerless have is the power to keep their word. I knew that someday, somewhere, an opportunity would present itself to me and I would fulfill the curse that I had sworn against my boss.

My first foray into fulfilling the curse was to purchase and to wear to work a completely see through blouse. It was a great day for me despite the fact that I was totally freaked out and frightened beyond any common sense! The guys who worked in the department usually spent most of their time ogling the breasts of my female co-workers as well as my breasts even when I was discussing business with them. Come ladies, you know the drill: you engage a male counterpart at work and the conversation normally begins with two pair of eyes staring intently at one another and then a pair of those eyes begin to wander and end up on a part of your anatomy, although one of those pairs aren't your two eyes. If the wandering eyes are caught in mid-perusal, the male worker's eyes dart quickly back to the female's eyes and once eye contact has been briefly re-established, the male's eyes will once again begin that slow glide down the female form until they come to rest once again upon her breasts.

On the day that I choose to wear my navy blue see-through blouse, that day should have been highlighted in the annals of female payback to men for all of the ogling we have to endure. I swept into work appearing to be unconcerned about my attire and more importantly unaware of the fact that I was wearing a piece of clothing that clearly revealed my naked breasts. I managed to greet every guy in the department with a big "Hello!" All of my female co-workers were aware of why I was wearing the blouse and each greeted me with a smile and thumbs-up to show their support. Every male I met almost choked as they struggled to maintain eye contact with me as they fought desperately to furtively but quickly look from my eyes to my chest. In the two years that I worked in that department, there had never been a day, prior to that day, where I received so much consistent eye contact from my fellow male employees. Even the one eared elephant guy, my boss, managed to keep his eyes glued on mine. And on that day of all days, my boss wasn't able to crack one foul joke in my presence. It was as if my boss had been struck dumb and I suppose that he had been, but the future held even greater surprises for him and greater delight for me. That day was a mere baby step in my design to pull off the ultimate coup de grace.

A few months had elapsed since my see through blouse day and a celebration was in the making for my boss' birthday. I volunteered to buy a gift for the boss and a cake for the celebration. The late 1960's were known as the days of love, peace and happiness. In keeping with the then current open attitude towards drugs, sex and rock and roll there were many places and shops where "hippies" sold their wares. On Santa Monica Blvd. in West Hollywood, just west of Beverly Hills, was a large old barn that housed talented young hippies who were extremely talented and produced incredible art. The talents ranged from tie-dyed clothing to intricate glass-blown pipes. The array of batik and tie-dyed clothing coupled with exotic candles, posters and a few items that today's law enforcement personnel would refer to as "drug paraphernalia" complimented the smoky smell of incense that permeated the air.

The barn was located just a few short blocks east of the data center where I worked. I actually loved walking into the location because it was a sensual delight. It was impossible not to be affected by the bright colors, the heady smells from incense burners all complimented by soothing sounds from fountains or soft rock background music.

I quickly found a perfect cake that was a mere four inches in diameter. I wandered about from stall to stall trying to find a gift that would be appropriate for the boss. Out of the corner of my eye I spied a unique candle shop. The shop was manned by a fresh faced young woman dressed in traditional hippie garb. Her eyes and skin were clear and sparkling, her hair pulled back from her Madonna like face. A sly smile kissed her lips as she became aware that I was a bit taken aback by the type of candles that she offered for sale. Can you imagine row after row of life sized penises? I managed to quietly suck in a deep breath of air before mustering enough nerve to ask this beatific vision that stood before me if these wax phalluses were for sale. Each candle was the exact physical representation of a male penis in every color from every race on earth. The young lady presented and reeked home spun wholesomeness from every aspect of her being and then she spoke to me. Her voice kind of tickled the base of your spine as the words tumbled from her perfect strawberry lips. Her description of how each candle was made was mildly titillating because as a clinician she described every detail of how to cast a wax mold using live male models.

The gong sounded loudly in my brain as I began to realize that before me stood the promised coup de grace! I bought a magnificent specimen, a specimen that was a little bigger than twelve inches long resting atop a four inch base. The four inches at the base was handy because it would be a perfect, snug fit for the top of the birthday boy's cake. And the capper for the Good Ole Boy from Arizona was that it was a big black wax penis! I simply floated back to the office with my purchases in tow as I anticipated the look on my boss's face when he was confronted with that big, black cock on his birthday cake. The thought of what he might be thinking, that is, his haphazrd thoughts as he was forced to blow out the candle was a dizzying thought for me. It didn't matter if I lost my job over this joke. This joke would make up for all the months of his unsettling and unnerving one eared elephant jokes and the constant teasing from him and the other guys in the department. It was heavenly to be able to keep my promise to him that one day: "I'm going to get you back, I promise!" to the blue-eyed, good-natured redneck who was my boss.

When I returned to the office with the goodies, I found a staff employee, our Georgia Peach, who just so happened to be a very attractive young lady from Georgia. The attributes of the Georgia Peach weren't missed by the boss who drooled silently over her on a daily basis. So it wasn't difficult for him to spend a little time with her in his office to keep him from being underfoot. I then made sure that all of the staff members, except for the Georgia Peach and the boss, were assembled in the staff lunch room. When everything and everyone was arranged, I sent one of the girls to fetch the boss and the peach from his office.

Ms. Georgia Peach preceded the boss into our assembly. Upon entering the doorway, she turned around and faced him and threw her arms around Boss Man's neck and planted the biggest, most suggestive kiss on his lips that I had ever witnessed. It's one of the few times that I ever saw the Boss Man blush. Off guard and slightly embarrassed, Boss Man entered the room and everyone began to sing "Happy Birthday" as someone turned out the lights. The birthday boy was standing kind of half-in, half-out of the doorway, leaning slightly forward in that hunk sort of lean when I approached him from behind with the magnificent lit penis candle lighting the darkness.

The candle on top of the cake was truly a sight to behold. The wax had begun to melt and run ever so slightly down the sides of the phallus. When the birthday boy turned around and faced me I deftly pushed the cake and candle under his nose and requested him to: "Make a wish and blow." He blushed even more than after receiving that kiss from the sexy Georgia Peach until he realized what was underneath his nose. The entire room erupted into laughter. Enough said! Just be aware that revenge can be really very sweet indeed!

I'm quite certain that my ex-boss still remembers that day of infamy and that his special gift from me made an impact on his future behavior because I don't think he ever teased me again with his stupid one one-eared elephant joke. He also didn't privately tell me any more off-color or lewd jokes unless we were in the company of both males and females. So gentle ladies who find yourselves being most uncomfortable around men and women who tell lively, bawdy sexual jokes; the lesson for the day is to find ways to stop a guy in his tracks when he says things you don't particularly like rather than to brutalize him and ruin his career, his life and to take away his livelihood for just being a guy.

One of the primary issues of the Feminist Movement should have been how to secure equal pay for women in the workplace. The point is that women and men should be paid the same for equal job performance rather than having a gliding salary scale based on the gender, race or the whim of a Human Resource professional. Unfortunately, in the liberated world of 2008, women's salaries still lag behind their male counterparts and part of the reason for this lag is due to how the feminists demanded equal rights in the workplace.

And in the midst of this great social mix of confusion are the goddesses. The goddesses are often times women who work simply because they need to fulfill some inner "career" need or to "find themselves." Most working goddesses don't have an economic necessity to earn money to support a family. Unfortunately, the media has largely focused its attention on the goddesses in the workplace rather than on normal women who represent every ethnic and lower to mid-level economic group who *have to* work to provide for their families.

As an ex-high school teacher I have had the opportunity to spend quite a lot of time with female students. Over the years I have been asked by several young female students if I would mind being interviewed about the birth of the women's rights movement in the workplace. One of the most insightful questions that emerge from "Women's Studies" classes is: "how have things changed for women in the workplace since you were my age?" Another supposed insightful and misguided question is: "Did you or do you still enjoy the freedom of being able to work and earn an income?" Goddesses have been spared the reality of what it means and feels like to come home exhausted from work five or more days a week and no goddess arrives home with more chores to complete before she can head off to bed. Goddesses have had the good fortune of being able to employ other women to clean their homes, iron their clothes, and to cook their food and sometimes, educate their children. The average female worker still works in jobs that compensate them with low salaries and few, if any opportunities for advancement. This professional stagnation can dampen attitudes and creates a damper when it comes to dreaming about future economic success.

I am certain that despite Oprah's and other talk shows popularity with women, there thousands of women across the nation who don't have equal access to achieving their dreams. Many of these women are desperately trying to hang onto the vestiges of their dreams. Some sit, mesmerized, in front of their television screens seeking that daily "fix" by slipping out of their reality and into the reality of the women who have achieved their dreams.

But, let's also be clear and admit that conditions in the workplace and in society at large have changed mostly for the well-educated and privileged women. These women would have risen to the top of their professions because of their social and/or cultural standing much like their male counterparts. The unfortunate thing is that many of the women who do manage to rise in the executive suite are often goddesses. Goddesses hate competition from other women.

American businesses, like goddesses, for the most part, are a social anachronism peppered with the sins of the past committed against women and minorities by the men who ran them because many of these men are often members of the powerful "Old Boys Club." The Old Boys Network didn't really begin as an exclusive group that barred women and minorities from its ranks. Goddess social structures mirror the Old Boys Network and are formed just like every other social group: people choose to associate with people that they know or share a common experience with and those experiences range from education institutions to social groups that encompasses church or country club membership.

Oddly enough, with all the jockeying for top the dog positions and economic remuneration, goddesses somehow seem to emerge from the competition at the top of the pack and claim their piece of the pie without disturbing a hair on their pretty little heads. The goddesses have been the phalanx of the new feminist movement but they have also lobbied to change exactly how men relate to women in the workplace. For want of a better descriptive word, let's call the goddesses who pushed for these social changes between men and women the Uptight Goddesses.

One of the biggest issues to be confronted by feminists in the workplace was the notion that some men and women want to play footsie with one another at work, whereas many female employees were the victims of sexual harassment by their male superiors. So, the feminists crafted guidelines that were supposed to help employers and female employees to avoid sexual harassment in the workplace. A pall generated by fear of sexual harassment lawsuits settled over corporate America and men, in particular, find it increasingly difficult to interact with the women they work with because of their fear of being unwittingly accused of sexual harassment. The feminists spurred by goddesses managed to censor male conduct towards women in the workplace.

So, what has evolved for most men in the workplace is a place filled with unseen landmines. The point is that if a woman is old enough to find and maintain a job shouldn't she also have learned how to ignore unwanted sexual innuendos from men just like she ignores the daily gossip at the water cooler? The rules really haven't changed all that much. The bottom line is that men should always keep their hands to themselves and women should ignore unwanted off-color comments and/or jokes from the office adolescent.

The Uptight Goddess class wants to not only censure the words that come out of a man's mouth but they would love to censure what men think. Over the years I've heard stories told about goddesses becoming enraged because an unfamiliar man, that was probably beneath their social status, had the audacity to compliment them. The sad fact of the matter is that many Uptight Goddesses embrace a false sense of prudery and many try to foist this faux prudery on the rest of society.

The bottom line for most men and a growing segment of modern young women is their need to satisfy their transient sexual desires. So, of course the workplace is a great place to meet people to satisfy those needs. And everyone is fully aware of what can happen if that sexual attraction turns aggressive between a superior and a line employee.

Corporate female climbers are also a part of America's corporate culture. These female climbers are women who deliberately choose to sleep their way to the top. Let it be said at this point that all goddess/divas are not rich or well-placed in society. In every economic/ethnic strata of society there are women who are card-carrying goddesses. Therefore, the workplace is not only populated by well-heeled, privileged goddesses but also by goddesses that dream of becoming powerful and wealthy goddesses. These 'climbers' have made it inordinately more difficult for talented women to gain recognition and advancement in the corporate world. Like older, wealthy men, corporations like to employ pretty, eager and young females that wish to rise quickly within an organization. And the quicker these young climbers attract an older, powerful man in the executive suite the quicker they'll assume the reins of power and forget who they were when they started. These goddesses also manage to forget an almost implied obligation to assist other women up the corporate ladder. Goddesses are not interested in helping other women who might bring substance and quality to their workplace.

Out of the Feminist Movement came the discordant cry from women that they wanted to be as sexually free as men to engage freely in sexual liaisons as men have for centuries. What modern feminists really wanted to gain in their quest for sexual autonomy with men was to garner male acceptance of their sexual desires to engage in and satisfy those sexual needs with whomever without guilt or recrimination for their actions.

So, the Feminist Revolution in the 1970's ushered in "out-loud" sexually liberated women who could no longer tolerate any men making either a veiled or a blatant sexual overture in the workplace. But wait: how can women be sexually liberated and also be unable to deal with 'out loud' male sexual desire? The point is, feminists wanted the ability to be sexually free but they also wanted the power not to be confronted with sexual desire from men that they didn't desire. So, a mere forty years after the most recent sexual revolution in America, the feminist movement has birthed a large population of sexually liberated, some well-paid female executives who somewhere along the way lost their ability to attract men. Many of these well-paid executive women, who share their life stories on shows like Oprah, claim to be clueless about how to attract men who might be their equal. Most of these women are so busy working and trying to climb the corporate ladder that their only source of information about how to "hook up" comes from the glossy pages of women's magazines. So for todays over thirty, high-powered executive female, just how does she complete her life with a man who is her equal? What to do...what to do?

Let's start with the premise that if men expressed admiration about a woman's body or the color of her hair or the turn of her ankle, the poor dumb thing would be chastised verbally because he had overstepped the boundaries established by feminists. In their quest to be competitive and be accepted by men as equals, feminists managed to sacrifice a subtle charm that women used to use to discourage unwanted male attention without offending or humiliating them. And then there are the 'liberated' women who experience a private joy whenever they are able to humiliate any man.

An offended goddess is something to be feared and please be aware that many men have lost their livelihoods because of a spurned goddess. Many sexual harassment lawsuits could have been settled amicably if the goddess had been satisfied with mere cash. For a lot of feminists, money just isn't enough. To garner full satisfaction for an uttered sexual suggestion, some women must also ruin the reputation of a man. A lot of goddesses prefer to perceive an innocent invitation from a man as harassment or sexual perversion. These are a few of the issues that exists today between men and women.

But since we're dealing with reality, it's time to really talk about sex in the workplace. Consensual workplace liaisons, (read sex with co-workers) should not be compared to an inappropriate and illegal situation where a superior coerces a line employee into a sexual relationship, or any other type of coercion that forces an employee to do anything that is against their moral or personal judgment. The facts are simple: there are predatory people in every profession. Race and gender are not factors to to try to establish predation. If an individual has been found to engage in predatory behavior in the workplace, then that person should lose something whether it be their livelihood or their reputation. On the other hand, in the interest of 'fairness,' all men and women should have the right to pursue friendly or sexual liaisons in the workplace in the workplace without fear of censure, if they dare. If grown adults would conduct themselves like mature adults, then, let the games begin. In a gesture to make life easier between male and female employees, there is just one rule that every employee should have tattooed on the back of their eyelids about workplace affairs: if you can't act like real adults then "no, means no!" To clarify what acting like an adult means if someone decides to have a workplace affair, then one big rule would be only engage in "kissy face" at home and never at the office. And if and when the relationship comes to an end, then only engage in the acrimony that accompanies most break-ups outside of the job. These are common sense suggestion and things that most adults should know.

With all things being equal and of course if all sociopaths decided to stay home and watch their DVD's or the soaps rather than go to work, then I sincerely believe that women wouldn't need protections from normal men in the workplace. The point is that grown women are not helpless and can't handle in the office what she easily handles in the local pub! Trust me: that damsel in distress hype died a long time ago along with the chastity belt.

Now, gentle readers, before you close the book and throw it across the room or into the trash bin, I am completely sensitive to the reality of sexual harassment in the workplace. I am probably more sensitive to the issue than most. My oldest daughter was clearly the victim of sexual harassment by a senior male employee. This individual was a senior executive and enjoyed preying on women. He tastes ranged from female customers to young female employees. The man had an unquenchable thirst for seducing females. My daughter was irrevocably marked by the experience. To this day, many years after the incident, my daughter cannot pass the place of her former employer without experiencing nausea and the shakes.

The incident unfolded like this. My daughter, who is extremely attractive, has long, naturally curly hair. When she's not working or going to school, she loves dancing at the upscale clubs on Sunset Blvd in West Hollywood. Her level of attractiveness, even by Southern CA standards, affords her a "pass go" card at the entrance of the trendy clubs. The bouncers consider her a draw for the paying male clientele.

By day, my daughter masquerades as a drone. On this fateful day she arrived at work on time as usual. An audit of her department was to take place by the senior VP. To my daughter's surprise, she was called into a small enclosed area of the office to speak directly with the senior VP about what he called "irregularities."

Once she entered the small enclosed area, the senior VP closed the door behind her. As the senior VP steeped towards her, my daughter stepped back, away from the man. He advanced towards her again and decided to assume a position of authority. "Mary, can you tell me why there is an inconsistency in these numbers on the receivables report?" My daughter moved towards the proffered report. As stepped towards the man to look at the report that he was holding, he reached out and caressed her curls that laid on one of her breasts. His action was followed by a smile. My daughter froze and then managed to shake out of the shock of the moment and managed to leave the room.

Words are so inadequate to describe her emotional and psychological response to this uncalled for transgression against her person. She had never entertained the thought that of willingly spending time with this person. He was at least twenty years her senior and physically repulsive. Once my daughter regained her composure, she reported the incident to her immediate supervisor and then to Human Resources. The icing on the cake of course came when my daughter realized that the corporation that employed them decided that the VP's actions were acceptable and that my daughter was expendable. An investigation was launched by the Board of Directors in an attempt to prove that my daughter had in fact entrapped the senior VP.

The response of the Board of Directors to a clear case of sexual harassment in the workplace is also a clear example of how the Old Boys Network has gone awry. The Board of Directors felt that their male senior VP and his flagrant behavior coupled with a previous blemished record of complaints from former employees and customers were all unimportant and insignificant to them. Therefore, the Board of Directors felt confident that the olive branch they offered to this miscreant would be fully supported and accepted by their idea of: "Boys will be boys!"

So, I am clearly not insensitive to true cases of sexual harassment, but I am also completely insensitive to grown women who can't seem to handle normal, everyday, male/female sex games and/or flirting that often occurs in the workplace. Unfortunately, in today's workplace, far too many women respond with far too much venom to men who genuinely only want to compliment them. This tense situation that exists between men and women in the workplace has spun completely out of control as evidenced by the backlog of sexual harassment lawsuits that fill court calendars.

There is one major problem that continues to persist in the workplace between men and women and that is the eternal goddess who responds inappropriately to normal male attention. Some of these women have an over-reaching self concept and many of them only respond to males who are well-placed economically and a power player. Regardless of which females respond negatively to male appreciation in the workplace and contrary to feminist beliefs, men should have the right to tell a woman that they admire her appearance. Simple? Well, at least that's the way it's supposed to work.

Working in the data processing center was an eye opener in that there were more consensual sexual liaisons on the rooftop parking lot than in most college dorm rooms. Maybe the proliferation of sexual liaisons at the data center was a consequence of people working the swing shift or possibly because the bank employed large numbers of sexually frustrated and unsatisfied men and women. Maybe having to work in such close proximity to one another, night after night, made the late lunch hour on the roof in closed, hot and steamy cars became so popular for late night sexual frenzy?

The time for sexual harassment lawsuits was twenty years in the future and not something anyone thought about in the late 1960's. That time frame occurred a few years before the "burn the bra" era. The late 1960's also found a lot of young people in the nation emotionally eclipsed by the love, peace, and happiness movement and of course everyone was "equal."

Somewhere along the line after the death knell sounded for the love peace and happiness generation the moral goddesses got it into their judgmental little heads that they were the only ones who knew what was right for the rest of us. They tried by influencing what our children listened to or watched. What resulted was that the goddesses decided that they knew what was best for our children. And because goddesses seem to be capable only of dealing with the lowest common denominator, our daily lives have been greatly impacted by zero tolerance and the "no-thinking" moral goddesses.

Once upon a time, there was a breed of women who managed to make most men feel like men. In other words, these women enjoyed being women and they enjoyed spending time with men who appreciated their femininity. These women were endowed with the physical attributes of women but they also possessed and radiated charm and warmth. Women in the past knew how to allow men to feel manly because their feminine personalities were a social construct that is now, almost extinct.. Some women in the distant past were able to deliver a lewd joke without making a man feel uncomfortable or dirty. The point is that jokes about sex or adult behavior are in the realm of adult humor and adult humor is not meant for children to hear, understand or participate in. And therein lays the rub for modern moralists sometimes revealed as goddesses. Some goddesses have appointed themselves as modern day moral cops. These morality goddesses want all interaction between men and women to be cleansed and sanitized and made palatable for the consumption of children.

Contrary to goddess think, it really is okay for adults to share off-color jokes with other adults. Bawdy and at times offensive humor is one of the side benefits of being an adult. Along with accepting the boundaries of adult humor comes the bold idea that women should also have the right to dress and to act in ways that please them, without having to worry about censure from feminists groups or goddesses. For some women, even today, sexy is just their style.

The feminists clearly haven't aided the climate that exists between men and women because they spearheaded and demanded legislation to brand male sexual appreciation of a woman as harassment. In this time of female liberation, far too many women are uncomfortable with the idea of being real sexual beings in an established relationship rather than the transient hook-ups that don't require commitment. The feminist movement spurred by goddesses has created a broad spectrum of sexual harassment that is responsible for tagging the most innocent of sexual interest from a man into coercion and rape.

Today's social landscape is populated by brass young women who are either too desperate in their search for male companionship or too dismissive. Think about it: today, many years after the impact of the feminist movement of the 1970's, guys still have to muster up enough courage to walk-up to an unknown woman to simply say "Hello!" And it has become a rare for many young men to meet a woman who is open to male advances without also expecting to receive some type of negative feedback in response to his interest. Most people with jobs who are single will meet most of their sexual prospects at work. Since people can meet good and bad prospects at work here is an example of "the bad."

When I was in my mid-thirties I worked for a man that can only be described as vile. He was a sexist and very possibly a racist. Now, here was a man who had no problem crossing barriers in the workplace with his female employees.

His physical qualities were the least of his problems. He was almost 5'6" tall, mid to late forties, balding with a slight pot belly. This man is one of the few men that I have encountered in my life that put the word "dirty" on par with sex. His whole persona was unpalatable and especially so when he attempted to make off-color remarks about sex. The only way that he related to women was through intimidation. Most of his conduct exposed his tendency to be mean and crude. For purposes of gifting him a name, let's call him the Troll

Let's begin by addressing the specifics of this odious situation. First of all, I don't have anything against short, bald men. And if I did have something against short, bald men, the loss would be mine. The truth is that I think that bald men are kind of sexy. There are men who bring a certain kind of je ne sais quoi to bald. And short? Well, I have been called a 'midgee' a lot in my lifetime so being a man being short isn't a repulsive idea to me or a relationship breaker. There is a certain, sensual appeal to smooth, supple, baldheads. But I digress. I was hired by this short, bald man to spearhead a new Loan Division in savings and loan institution located in a nearby beach community. I could never think of the Troll as a gentleman because, in my experience, the Troll was never a gentleman in any sense of the word during our brief, but turbulent relationship.

After the Troll hired me, I was concerned with learning how the organization functioned and how to best launch this new division to ensure a sound foundation and profits. The newly formed division had three employees, the Troll, his male assistant and I. Both the Troll and his assistant had worked together previously for a cut-throat finance company, before the migrated to work in a more controlled lending environment without the cut-throat tactics. The "loan" department also had a central clerical staff of ten to service the consumer loan division that was also under the Troll. Neither the Troll nor his assistant had ever made a commercial loan (think short term business loan and not just used car loans or cut-throat second trust deed loans) because they had only worked for finance companies. Neither of the two men had experience in nor training in bank lending therefore, neither man had the critical lending experience in short-term business financing to launch a new division. The Troll's primary responsibility, before my hire, was to expand the S & L's second trust deed portfolio, to make auto loans and collect on delinquent accounts. Neither man understood the underlying principles of how to structure substantial business loans (loans in excess of a twenty-five million dollars that had to be repaid, plus interest, in less than a year) to clients without using some kind of asset to secure the debt.

After a brief settling in, the boss, the assistant and I adapted a daily ritual that was implemented by the boss. Everyday, somewhere between 4:30 and 5:00 PM, the assistant, the Troll and I would convene in the Troll's office to discuss new loans and the performance of current loans while imbibing a half gallon of vodka. I'm not certain about other professions, but as a Corporate Banker one of the skills all lending executives needed to cultivate was to be able to imbibe large amounts of alcohol without appearing drunk. You have to understand that bankers back in the day controlled the purse strings to lend millions of dollars and that every business lunch or dinner was accompanied by the de rigueur cocktail. I kind of think that if bankers conducted business meetings at breakfast that mimosas would have been mandatory the de rigueur drink.

At the time, as a female, I worked in a profession that was mostly populated by males and if there were women in the field they had to learn how to drink just like the "fellas." God knows that a woman's career could have rested on her not passing out at one of those drinking fests as surely as her career also rested on her ability to make loans that repaid. Learning how to "hold my liquor" was an unspoken part of my job description as well as that I had to have superior lending skills coupled with expertise in structuring those loans in order to successfully launch that new division.

One of the oddest things about working for the Troll was his choice of employees. As stated previously the S & L was located in a southern CA beach community. Most beach communities in So Cal are populated mostly by white people. The majority of the employees who worked for this S & L were white and yet the Troll's clerical staff was completely comprised of black females except for a lone white, gay male.

The Troll rewarded the staff by taking them for dinner and drinks twice monthly at a local marina. Occasionally, like most institutions, there would be staff office parties and employees from other departments would visit different floors to explore the people in different departments for possible hook-ups. As the flow of liquor increased, the staff members became less inhibited and grown-ups were suddenly transformed into teenagers in hot pursuit of exchanging spit with a relative stranger in a forbidden environment.

Within months after I was hired, the Troll made it abundantly clear to me that he had had every intention to bed me. His intention and revelation made me positively queasy. It took a few months for me to gain my professional confidence in this new environment and once I did, I began to focus on the Troll and his incessant sexual badgering. After months of acrimony and building rage, the taste of bile rose in my mouth whenever I was near the man for any reason and I made it abundantly clear that he would never have sex with me, even after death. I am aware that I was brutally honest with the man but there was never any emotion or gesture from me that would have encouraged him to chase my skirt. The Troll became a pest. He openly accused me of having sex with my male clients as well as the various loan brokers who provided me with possible customers. Simply because I worked for the man he assumed that my entire life, and that included my private life as well, was somehow open to his inspection. As his accusations increased about whom I was sleeping with so did his amorous advances. I found myself constantly moving away from his hands. If he found the opportunity to "accidentally" rub up against me in close corners as he passed by, my stomach would jolt and the stench of his after shave lingered on my clothes. All the signs were there; there was absolutely no way for me to avoid an open confrontation with my boss about my personal boundaries that he constantly breached.

I had just returned from a trip to Ft Lauderdale Florida to check on a commercial venture that needed start-up funds. I hadn't had any sleep in over thirty-six hours and I was supposed to report to work at eight for a staff meeting. The Troll called my home about 6:30 that morning. He began to interrogate me about who I had slept with on my brief trip. I managed not to snap but I did inform him that I wouldn't be able to get to work before 10:00 AM. He paused briefly and tossed the idea around in his head. I told him that my return flight had been rough and that I had one of my classic headaches. I managed to purr into the phone: "If you can see your way clear to allow me to report late, I'd love to take a walk with you when I arrive so that we can discuss my trip?" I could smell the cogs turning in his bald, cretin head. He waited almost a full thirty seconds before responding with: "why, yes of course. See you at ten."

Needless to say, I was livid. I knew that it was time for me to put the Troll in his place. I was also aware that I could lose my job because the Troll was a vindictive and mean man.

I choose to wear a black power suit with black stockings and high heels. When I arrived at the office at ten I was all business. I stuck my head into his office and asked the Troll if he would mind taking a walk, right now. A smile creased his face and a bit of spittle formed in the corner of his mouth. He nodded and stood, walking towards the door. I backed and began to head for the elevator. I knew that if I delivered my planned speech to the Troll on the premises that he could claim that I was insubordinate and fire me on the spot. Taking a walk off premises made it appear as if we were friends.

As I existed the building I glanced behind me and caught the Troll's hungry eyes devouring my body. A shiver of revulsion ran up my spine but I continued to walk in front of him until we were off bank property. The Troll informed me that nothing of great consequence had happened during the morning meeting. As we rounded the corner away from the bank I stopped and turned towards the Troll.

It was almost impossible for me to control my anger. The Troll enjoyed the coming storm. He knew that he had pricked and upset me, and like most emotional juvenile people, the Troll elected to experience some type of contact with me rather than settling for no contact at all.

The confrontation began with me asking him about: "Exactly why do you think that you have the right to question me about who I have sex with?" A smile creased his vile lips. I continued: "You know that you're walking a tight rope on this issue! Let's face it; if I were John (his male assistant) and you walked into your office and caught me screwing your secretary on your desk, you'd clap me on the back and say 'way to go.' And walk out. But because you want to think that I'm having sex with customers you feel that you have the right to question my morals! Well, you're wrong. It's none of your damn business if I'm sleeping around or not. If you think you can prove that I am, and if the activity is detrimental to the bank, then fire me! Otherwise, get off my back. Don't ever ask me again if I'm sleeping with someone, not even with my husband! If this issue is ever brought up again, I'm going straight to personnel. Do you understand me?" I turned and walked away from him and back to my office.

Despite the Troll's aggressive sexual overtones to me and his veiled threats, I managed to maintain my dignity if not my job. The point is - each of us (read women) has the power to deal with unpalatable situations that might arise, irrespective of rape, in the workplace. Women who fake being incapable of dealing with rudeness, crudeness or open sexuality from their male co-workers literally bore the hell out of me and a whole lot of men. The bottom line: these kinds of women should just grow up. If a woman can't differentiate a compliment from a salacious innuendo then this lady needs more alone time and should consider working in a nunnery. If the lady so chooses to work and if she is offended by sex talk or crude jokes, then the dear lady needs but to remember that she has every right just to walk away from the situation, even if it's her boss that is acting inappropriately.

It took a few decades for me to learn this fact but I finally learned that men don't really have it any easier than women do in the workplace. The reality is there are few spots at the top of any corporation, even for talented, hard-working men or women. In the heat of competition to rise to the top, both men and women must possess talent, be well-connected and lucky enough to be at the right place at the right time to make it to the top slot in any profession or industry.

If feminists nationwide were able to admit, out loud, that every woman who has claimed sexual harassment or rape in the workplace wasn't actually harassed or raped then the divide that separates men and women could be mended. If feminists could find it in their hearts to admit that there is a breed of women who have no problem with lying about being raped or harassed by a guy just for money, then men and women could begin to re-approach one another with mutual respect. If feminists admitted that there are some women who claim rape and/or harassment aren't really interested in equality or equal pay for all women, but are only interested in securing their financial futures at the expense of decency and fairness, then maybe the scale of justice can tip back towards the center and men and women can begin to live peacefully with one another. If and when feminists admit that there are women who hate men as much as some men hate women and that many of these man-hating women will only be content when innocent men are locked away behind bars; then that divide that is almost impassable between men and women will continue to separate them.

The overwhelming sad fact is that the numbers of ruthless women who are intent on economically crippling men and corporations appears to be increasing. These female sociopaths appear to be on the rise and are not being "outed" by feminists groups but are instead being defended by feminists organizations and powerful female attorneys. Most feminists have adopted a reflexive, unthinking and emotional response to rape charges committed by men. Harassment and physical abuse charges result in feminists being worked-up into a frenzied rage. The sad fact is that all women, like all men can't be trusted to act honorably. Although the media may say that women "misstates issues" while men lie, the fact is that both groups have members that tell lies and both groups have their fair share of selfish and manipulative individuals. Until these facts impact how "truth" is handled between these two groups, then men and women will view each other across the abyss with distrust.

The Passive/Aggressive Female
Chapter 5

One definition for passive/aggressive personality disorder is: "Passive/ aggressive personality disorder is a chronic condition in which a person seems to passively comply with the desires and needs of others, but actually actively resists them, becoming hostile and angry." So, to take another step off of a very high cliff, I would wager that there are more passive/aggressive women in the world than passive/aggressive men. The assumption is based on the inherent acculturation that happens to most women. Women were exclusively assigned a secondary status of importance in most societies. Even today, in many modern societies, women are still required to act and respond in passive/aggressive ways just to survive in male dominated cultures.

The reality of growing-up female in the world often times means that a whole lot of women successfully learn how to swallow and hide their true feelings from the people in their lives. Similar to other learned behaviors, the passive/aggressive behavior is a learned activity that most little girls learn from their mothers, grandmothers or other powerful women in their lives. Most men will probably find this next statement incomprehensible but many women do not run their mouths constantly from sunup to sundown. In fact there are millions of women across the face of the world who don't know how to give voice to their feelings.

Many women have learned over the years how to mask their emotions by following an internal play book that safely charts their emotional lives through the dangerous emotional and sometimes physical dangers that surround them. The people in most women's, husbands, children and other family members, lives take priority over their personal needs. Being concerned with the needs of others as a consistent diet, often at the expense of their own needs and well-being often bankrupts a woman's perspective and the only way that she can respond to the world is through passive/aggressive activities. Many women have never considered the possibility that they have the right to be happy based on their desires and choices. Therefore the American female is a fortunate woman indeed. But make no mistake; even though American women are the freest and the most privileged women in the world, there are thousands of American women who live their lives as passive/aggressive females because of either their culture or for survival. In other words, many women live their lives with a basic assumption about what they think should make them secure and happy and many women are woefully bereft of the skills required that would ensure their security and happiness. Too many women simply accept that the source of their happiness resides in the happiness of their children or their spouses. It is obvious that many of these women, lost souls to be sure, are slaves to their families and are, at their core, selfless women who could never be mistaken or confused with being a goddess.

Over the years I have spoken with many women about goddesses and how their lives have been impacted by them. I have been told by a few women that the goddess complex, in their eyes, is an outward expression of the insecurity and fear that lurks somewhere in the emotional make-up of the goddess personality and as such, that goddesses shouldn't be blamed for their mean behaviors. But the truth is that insecure women do have a tendency to be passive/aggressive out of insecurity while goddesses tend to be emotionally aggressive and mean not out of insecurity but out of their desire to acquire power through manipulation or by hurting others. Some goddesses may in fact pretend to be passive/aggressive simply to feign emotional passivity when expedient or necessary to further their agendas.

Goddesses have been 'schooled' for years on how to effectively manipulate the people in their lives for their personal benefit. If a goddess is unhappy, she makes sure that her unhappiness is telegraphed to everyone around her in a dramatic way that most people who are sensitive to emotional currents scramble about trying to find someway to try to alleviate the goddess's displeasure. Just examine the oft repeated/accepted statement: "If the woman of the household is unhappy, then everyone in that household is unhappy!" This unexamined statement was probably initially spoken by a miffed goddess who quickly noted that everyone around her was trying to assuage her feelings.

It's almost impossible to mistake a normal female for a goddess. The normal female spends a tremendous amount of personal time fearing rejection and censure from the people in her life. To compound the situation for the normal female she also fears rejection, rather censure from other women. Without a doubt, many of the women that instill fear in the normal female are often goddesses.

Little girls from every hue and creed learn very early, primarily from their mothers, how to respond to their world. Some little girls learn early that they aren't as important in the scheme of things as their fathers, brothers and all men in general. Many young girls identify emotionally with their mothers. Whenever their mother telegraphs emotionally that she has been rebuffed by her husband, the emotionally aware child feels her mother's emotional pain. Little girls are open to and emotionally aware of the otherwise buried, very alive emotional tremors that erupt splinter and continue to fissure inside the topsy-turvy emotional world of their mothers. So, as the constant emotional diet of insults and recrimination fly from fathers to wives little girls that live in that household are keenly aware of the deep emotional recesses that many women strive to hide from the onslaught of disapproval that impugns their character, scars their souls and makes them question their basic right to simply be human.

Unfortunately, far too many little girls find themselves living with a built-in role model who has been emotionally and sometimes physically broken by other people. Many women learn to bury their true feelings and emotions as a reflex for survival. Many women live their lives by living in denial about the how much they feel rejection rather than suffer the affects of self-recrimination. Countless women have learned the fine art of 'disappearing' just to avoid disapproval or any other type of negative emotional from another person. For the emotionally bruised woman, any one of a host of implied failings can trigger tears or complete withdrawal.

For the woman who shares her life with an abusive man if the house wasn't properly cleaned, or if the dinner was under or overcooked or not cooked at all because of illness, and of course if the children are surly, unwilling and impolite when daddy dearest decides that he has a spare five minutes to finally spend with them, each one is the ignition point for an explosive and violent encounter. Little girls and truthfully all children are so painfully aware of the quick-silver emotions that flit through the air between adults and especially whenever daddy's attention innocently wanders towards a thinner, more physically appearing woman. And that child is also equally emotionally keyed into mommy's fleeting emotion of feeling threatened or unconcerned by her husband's natural response to another attractive female. If the child "feels" that mommy is threatened, that child mightl grow-up feeling threatened in similar circumstances. Similarly, if the mom is unthreatened and doesn't emotionally respond to the situation, then the child learns not to overreact to similar natural encounters with other people.

Learning to mask emotions is a learned female trait that occurs many years before women learn to fake orgasms in order to keep the peace in their homes. For many women, faking their emotions can be enhanced by flashing one of those nervous, disarming smiles or those infectious, unsuppressed giggles day after day, year after year, decade after decade until it becomes second nature. In many cases, this disarming behavior becomes the dominant personality trait of a woman who is completely uncomfortable with herself. The smile, that engaging totally human response, is also the earmark of the masking process that many women develop to hide their true emotions and feelings.

For many women the effects of having to constantly submerge their true emotions results in some women becoming master procrastinators and many are unable to make decisions about the simplest things that affect their daily lives. Women who manage to appear to be model housewives and mothers can suddenly, after years of exhibiting perfection to the outside world, begin to exhibit drastic signs of inefficiency within their homes. Lurking, unspoken problems can begin to emerge, benignly, and appear as a personality quirk of a once efficient and perfect wife where checks begin to bounce for non-sufficient funds in the checking accounts or charge purchases are denied due to being over-limit or unpaid. In a home where home cooked meals were once the norm, home-cooked meals are routinely replaced by prepared meals from the Boston Market, Dominoes Pizza or a constant flow of fast food items from "Mickey D's," Kentucky Fried Chicken, or Wendy's. Sometimes the wife will unintentionally forget to pick up her husband's weekly laundry or maybe she forgets to take his shirts and suits to be cleaned.

Independently, each of the foregoing incidents could simply point to an overworked and overburdened woman trying to run a household. Collectively, the log of her missed chores could be the signs of a wife and mother who has begun her descent into a world of inner chaos and pain. The once perfect wife and mother struggles desperately to accomplish the most simple of daily tasks while she simultaneously tries to find something that is meaningful to her in her life. Under the sometimes perfect surface, the woman is aware and afraid of her own disconnect and many women begin to self medicate in an attempt to improve their moods or to steady their nerves as they try to fight against the swirling black waves of doubt and fear that threatens their very sanity.

The roots of this type of submerged and often ignored silent dialogue that occurs all too often in women can be traced back to their pre-teen days. When little girls begin elementary school, most are geared up and eager to learn about their world and most little girls expect to meet and make new friends. As in most things that involve human beings, little girls gravitate towards other little girls because everyone feels more secure with people they are most like. In elementary school, in every class there is always one little girl who becomes the center of attention of other little girls. Sometimes a little girl becomes the center of attention in elementary school on her road to becoming a goddess, innocently, because this little girl out of all the other little girls in class just so happens to also be the teacher's pet. These little girls are almost always the most self-assured and outgoing students in the entire class.

Although some little girls become ostracized by other little girls in elementary school, more often or not at this age, most little girls seem to find other "acceptable" female classmates to play with during lunch, recess and after school. Of course little girls at this age get their feelings hurt from time to time and many tears are shed but most of these encounters are benign and the pain of rejection, which is generally short-lived, disappears quickly. Maybe part of the reason for the quick recovery from rejection for these little girls is that so many elementary school students' activities are planned by moms. Most mothers of elementary school children manage to throw parties that include every student in a classroom just to ensure that no one feels left out. And even though elementary schools have their share of little girls who are shy and on the road to becoming a passive/aggressive personality, elementary school is rarely the place where people make life-long enemies.

But middle-school is the place where passive/aggressive female behaviors are honed into a science. Middle-school is the birthplace of "mean girls." And a lot of mean girls appear to start off as being passive/aggressive personalities. It is important to understand that part of being passive/aggressive, whether male or female, is not being able to be yourself comfortably, especially around other people. Being a normal human being living a normal life it is very hard to think that some people are just born mean. In American culture it is widely accepted that there are mean children and mean men, but most people in America find it difficult to entertain and accept that there are mean women who purposefully adversely affected their lives.

Middle-school is the place where pre-teen girls learn to use an extremely potent weapon, gossip, against other girls. The art of gossip is technically a passive/aggressive behavior and some young girls begin to hone their gossip and back-stabbing skills in middle school. Middle school seems to be a particularly fertile environment where "mean girls" seem to gain emotional strength and power over other girls by flexing these well budding, deadly skills to annihilate their competition. Novice "mean girls" sharpens their skills simply by choosing an innocent target to humiliate in their quest to be popular. Mean girls in middle school appear to expand their special brand of nastiness by sabotaging the plans and goals of their enemies but also the plans of their so-called friends. For some unexplained reason, a lot of mothers whose daughters are mean girls manage to ignore or "tsk-tsk" the real harm that their little darlings wreak on other girls. The fact that moms receive numerous complaint phone calls about distraught girls who have undergone some form of cruelty because of "mean girls" and the behavior continues points to the undeniable fact that many of these mothers just don't care that they are raising mean girls. What are the chances that the mothers of middle school mean girls were once mean girls themselves and still are?

Middle school is also the place where elementary school friends' splinter into new groups. Middle school is the place where race and ethnicity become important and in schools where there is one dominant or single race, economics and class begin to separate and influence groups. The 'hot girl' syndrome also springs to the forefront in middle schools. The people who used to be the closest friends in elementary school sometimes morph into being your worst nightmare in middle. And to make matters worse, most social gatherings, like a girls night sleepover, can culminate with an innocent utterance of an ever so private secret to a 'friend,' that always manages to leak-out to the group during a rigorous game of "Truth or Dare." The secrets that leaked out during "Truth or Dare" seem to always to turn up as gossip during lunchtime.

The lunch tables are always full of laughing students and the mean girl cliques look around furtively for a likely target to become the butt of their jokes and when the target is spied their voices lower and morph into snickers as they stare and do everything except point at their latest victim. The victim is of course completely aware of this unwanted attention and the victim almost always wishes that she could crawl away from or be able to fall into a very deep hole that mercifully opens up when summoned, just to hide from all those mean, prying eyes. This heart wrenching scene is played out daily all across American middle school campuses as groups of young girls' huddle together giggling, laughing and trashing the reputations of other young girls who may or may not be present.

To reiterate, a lot of parents, mothers in particular, find ways to excuse this type of poor, mean spirited behavior practiced by their middle school aged daughters with: "Oh, that's kids stuff. Better to stay out of it and let them solve it." The truly disaffected mother responds with: "Kid shit!" and closes her mind to doing something about the tortuous social situation for someone else's kid. Most adults have managed to forget all about what it was like for them when they attended middle school and most parents can easily say and many believe that this type of behavior is acceptable because "these are just kids." The accepted "just kids" syndrome that afflicts far too many parents also embraces the idea that this type of unacceptable behavior engaged in by a young person will, in the future, miraculously disappear as a character flaw when the bully or the mean girl graduates from high school. The sad truth is that this type of ingrained abusive behavior becomes an even more entrenched behavior pattern as the goddesses, read mean girl, matures and finds themselves in the world of adults.

The behavior of mean girls can be compared to a junior science experiment although the steps of the 'experiment' aren't logically thought out before a mean girl or a group of mean girls begin to launch a targeted attack. Sometimes, a group of mean girls decide to attack another girl on the spur of the moment. Perhaps the clique spies someone wearing an outfit that they decide is comical looking or simply something that they would never choose to wear. The worst offense is for a non-clique member to commit is to wear the exact same outfit currently being worn by a member of the clique.

Most girls can surely remember the sting of walking down the hallway or into the cafeteria in our local middle school with the hair on the back of our necks prickled in response to the hard-to-miss silence that suddenly cloaked the entire hallway. That numbing silence was pierced by the hiss of whispers that shocked like the sound of breaking glass as we struggled not to just bolt from the coming assault of stares and snickers from the other students. How many times have young girls suffered from this type of unspoken assault on or about their person without apparent reason? Of course we have all been taught the familiar but untrue proverb: "sticks and stones may break my bones but words can never harm me," a proverb that is supposed to lessen the all too painful sting of words that stick like glue to our self-worth. And parents that admonish their kids with the familiar "Just, get over it!" are out of touch with just how hurtful words can be.

The truth is, words can and do hurt most people far more than inflicted physical pain and words leave much deeper and longer-lasting, unseen scars. The pain and after affects of physical pain begins to fade as time passes, that is, physical trauma disappears in much the same way as women 'forget' the pain associated with childbirth or how children forget the shock of pain that accompanies a broken bone and fades over time. Most physical traumas mercifully fade, on the other hand, negative and/or hurtful words are often emotionally ingested unwillingly by the recipient, and these words often create fragility in the underlying psyche of the victim. Some words that wound deeply are often accepted unwittingly by the victim as an accurate evaluation of their self worth.

Afterwards, the victim often finds it impossible to dislodge or remove the emotional sting of the spoken negative judgment from their emotional make-up. Mean girls and grown-up adult mean girls' transit in snide verbal assaults against other girls, other women and occasionally men.

First of all, mean girls don't just wake-up one day and decide to create a clique of mean girls to be mean to other people; at least not typically. Mean girl behavior in middle school begins first as a game that requires the participants to make someone else feel visibly uncomfortable. What mean girls seem to miss, or maybe they are clearly uninterested in understanding is the fact that the pain that they cause other girls to feel, in their desire to have fun at someone else's expense, is reprehensible behavior. Mean girls really don't care that other girls are not interested in playing their petty, mean girl ego games and they are not the least disturbed by the fact that some girls are really interested in forging friendships without making other people jump through hoops just to be their friend.

The behavior of most mean girls is animalistic in nature because they seek to draw emotional blood from their victims. Once the mean girl clique draws blood (think of Steven King's infamous <u>Carrie</u>), many mean girls experience a sense of euphoria after they have wounded another victim. That lone emotional high can be similar to that first rush of excitement that is felt when an animal draws that first blood in an attack. More accurately, for the budding mean girl, that first rush of endorphins that spread throughout her bloodstream after her first emotional assault is the middle school mean girl's first experience with true power. Once a group of mean girls target a victim and that victim responds either visibly or emotionally to their rejection or ridicule as evidenced by the victim collapsing into tears as the group experiences a sense of triumphant glee that spreads like wildfire throughout the 'pride.' The intoxication of their senses intensifies as the group begins to tentatively demean the victim and progresses to a skillful dissection of everything that is personal. The attacks always seem to focus on how someone's hair is styled or the pitch and tone of voice or simply their mode of dress or brand of shoes. Of course the attacks always end with the melodic, out-loud verbal insult like "What a dumb ass!"

If the victim's hair and make-up aren't always flawless (and who's is?) or if her choice of shampoo, body washes, perfume etc. are somehow unacceptable then the newly appointed scent captains emotionally pummels the victim by their peals of derisive laughter and hard to ignore snickers. As the group of mean girls successfully target more victims and earn high marks for emotionally disabling other girls just "because," the clique endeavors to undertake an expansion project where they can practice their cruelties on a much larger scale. Their attacks become ever more personal and begin to focus on the victim's home, their older/ younger siblings and some may begin to push the envelope by making snide and catty remarks about the victim's family or their economic status in the community. Like the currently embraced, nothing is off-limits culture in the United States nothing is off-limits to these mean girls. Everything is fair game to be used by these budding goddesses as weapons against chosen victims and there isn't a vestige of pity or sanctuary for the victim from the clique. Many parents of mean girls will cluck and say that the victims need to "man-up," and often the victim of choice is a passive person without any aggressive tendencies.

The only real relief that a victim can expect from a mean girl is for some other poor girl to become the target. Salvation for the victim often arrives in an unlikely form; that is, one of the accepted members of the clique inexplicably becomes the object of derision. The newly chosen victim is almost always a "hanger on," a fringe member of the group without power but yet enjoys few benefits of being an inside clique member. The "hanger-on" knows that she was accepted into the group without the expectation of receiving respect from the other clique members. The hanger-on's value is limited and her association with the clique is marginal. The hanger-on is usually the girl who blunders about and commits unwitting faux pas that sets the top diva's teeth chattering and in turn, often becomes the new, unwilling victim.

This ostracized member becomes the object of derision by her almost embracing clique and yet, this hanger-on is oddly in the group for a special kind of up-close and personal dissection that leads to above par meanness from her fellow clique members. The sycophant accepts the mistreatment from the clique members in the false hope that she will be able to regain her standing as a full-fledged mean girl. To re-earn her stripes and possible re-admittance to the group, the ostracized victim has to bring the group a new, fresh blood. The cycle of meanness is indeed vicious and almost never-ending because the possibility of intervention by teachers or parents almost never occurs. The reason is that parents and teachers obviously have more pressing and glaring problems to address than worrying about girls simply being mean to one another. And as the parents and adults in the lives of mean girls cleave to the age-old habit of letting kids deal with their own social problems without adult intervention, the mean girls are able to freely practice unparalleled meanness and emotional bullying against others while teenage suicides escalate. The survivors of these unnecessary tragic losses of life spend years trying to regain their moorings and sensibilities about how such an irresponsible tragedy could have ever occurred.

Passive/aggressive females are notorious for behaviors that devolve all too quickly into cruelty. Two pre-teen girls meet in middle school quite by accident. One is a newly transferred student from another near-by city and school district and the transplanted young girl is therefore friendless and completely unknown at the new school. The story is enhanced by the fact that there is another female student who is transferring from elementary to middle school. The transfer student has always attended schools in the city and the same school district since first grade. This student is also friendless because the move from elementary school to middle school also meant that she lost all of her friends because of the formation of new cliques that just so happens to revolve mostly around racial identity. Remember now that middle school is the place where kids begin to break certain bonds. Some of those broken bonds are internal ones tied to self-identification and as the middle school student changes externally and internally the internal bonds are in a state of constant flux. Seeming maturation also causes the young to break bonds with their parents based on a transient need to flee the security of their confined nests that are inextricable tied to their parents. The process of young people beginning to break their bonds with their parents begins with their parents being completely struck dumb. Translation: most pre-teens believe that they are far smarter than their old foggy parents. Eventually these middle school children come to the realization that their parents are a source of major embarrassment to them based on such subtleties such as how their parents dress or even something as innocuous as how their parent might say "hello" to them in the morning.

Science has exposed and touted the wonders of hormones in humans few have taken the time to elucidate on the fact that hormones also appear to render most pre-teens crazy. Anyone that has the fortitude, patience and stamina to endure being a middle school teacher or administrator for longer than a year should not only earn a high six or seven figure annual salary, but these tortured souls should also receive regular all expense paid vacations to any place their hearts desire. Teaching in middle school is like stepping into unsupervised monkey cage at the zoo.

In middle school the passive/aggressive goddess in training spends her time being discontent over the fact that she isn't good enough or can't measure up to becoming involved with the reigning popular group. Rather than cultivating healthy relationships with other girls who desperately want just to belong and to have one, true friend, the passive/aggressive goddess-in-training will typically strike up relationships with the "nice" girls on campus. Nice girls in middle school are girls who want to 'belong' but not at the cost of sacrificing their core of being decent human beings. Unlike goddesses-in-training, nice girls would never think of trying to control or dictate what choices other girls should make and nice girls never require someone to act in a certain, defined way. The good news is that nice girls are simply looking for friends that may, in the future, just turn out to be life-long friends. But middle school for nice girls is a tough place to be because being in middle school means that a person's worth as a human being is based on whether or not that person is a member of that end all, be all group better known as the popular group.

Therefore, middle school for a whole lot of young girls is a very uncomfortable place to be. To make matters worse, if you just so happen to be a really unlucky but nice girl, and you happen to fall into a relationship with a passive/aggressive goddess-in-training, odds are that Ms. Nice Girl will spend most of her time in and out of class trying to understand exactly "why" she is always so miserable. After awhile, Ms. Nice Girl is able to ascertain that she is most miserable whenever she is engaged with Ms. Submerged Goddess friend.

In middle school it is difficult for most "nice" girls to understand that they are involved in relationships with what in reality is a budding passive/aggressive goddess. As a person in a relationship with a passive/aggressive girl, the nice girl will eventually conclude that her new passive/aggressive friend insults her regularly about the most fundamental of issues like the nice girl's perceived latent or exposed sexuality that is inexplicably tied to whether or the nice girl will grow up to be a hard-drinking loser, slut. Maybe Ms Submerged Goddess decides to reveal to her nice friend what she "feels" will be the nice girl's future on a dark, cold and gloomy morning at school.

This revelation happens not as a gesture of friendship but simply because the Submerged Goddess feels the need to bond with someone in her own sick way and the only way that the passive/aggressive can only bond is by deeply wounding another person. The nice girl, hungry for acceptance has managed to ignore all of the not so subtle slights that her passive/aggressive friend has sent her way simply because the nice girl deludes herself into thinking that her passive/aggressive 'friend' offers her complete acceptance and warmth. What ensues is a cutting diatribe from the Submerged Goddess. Words fall from the Submerged Goddess's mouth like frozen honey: "Exactly how can you think that you're ever going to be anything more than a slut and a loser?" The nice girl feels as if the words flung at her by the Submerged Goddess are like shards of glass forcefully hitting against her bare skin. But these hurtful words are also the cold dash of reality desperately needed by the nice girl, words that immediately slam the victim back into the harsh reality of middle school life and the terrors that live there.

So, back to the saga of the nice girl and the Submerged (passive/ aggressive) Goddess: one day the two outcasts meet and find it easy to mingle because both are of mixed race heritage and both are lost in the vast sea that is the harsh reality of middle school. The two girls develop a fast friendship based on their mutual insecurities and needs. Middle school for these two outcasts is a landscape filled with invisible landmines and neither is experienced in avoiding the eventual explosions that are expected in a place that is manned by raging hormones and crazed young people trying to gain their independence from authority. Both girls are intelligent and attractive. One of the girl's appears to be emotionally stronger than the other and her strength allows her to cut through the ingrained adolescent habits of indecision and constant embarrassment because this girl makes most of the moves necessary to cement this budding relationship.

The emotionally stronger girl is a nice girl although she is like most other young girls in that she is still attracted to the popular group. Let's face it, the popular girls are the ones who always seem to be having fun and the popular girls are always surrounded by other popular and attractive people. Our nice girl, let's name her the Non Goddess, is locked out of the popular cliques because she is friendly, wholesome, honest and open about her thoughts and desires in life. The newly transferred student, let's name her La Transfer Goddess for the moment, is painfully quiet, withdrawn and only chooses to spend time with the Non Goddess rather than be alone in that crazy place known as middle school.

The Transfer Goddess is also a submerged passive/aggressive goddess that is completely aware that it is far worse for a person to be alone than for her to spend time with the Non Goddess. The Transfer Goddess also longs to be involved with the popular group but her fear stymies her efforts because she fears being unmasked and identified as a loser. There is absolutely nothing worse for a middle school student than to be judged as a loser by their peers. For the majority of adolescents, being a loser is worse than dying because being a loser means certain death in the realm of middle school society.

So, the Transfer Goddess morphs into the Submerged Goddess and she spends most of her free time at school and most of her free time away from school with the Non Goddess just to fill the empty hours. The newly minted Submerged Goddess literally chafes at being around the sparkling and outgoing personality of the Non Goddess. The Submerged Goddess either cannot or will not pry herself away from her self-imposed shell that also keeps her from being a real human being. Therefore, the Submerged Goddess must devise a plan to sabotage the only friend she has managed to make at her new school simply because she can and that is the only power that she has; the power to destroy.

The Submerged Goddess begins to subtly attack La Non Goddess. The Submerged Goddess begins by utilizing a classic female tactic, total and complete silence. Most women learn at some time in their lives that if they use silence for a sustained period of time that most people respond to their imposed silence, immediately. The Submerged Goddess, like most other passive/aggressive women, manages to emotionally upset and unbalance the Non Goddess because of her pointed use of silence. The tactic of silence almost always yields the same result when unleashed against either sex: the receiver of the silent treatment almost always responds because, intuitively, they know that something is wrong. They feel that once the silent treatment has been put into play that they are solely responsible for whatever transgression has occurred. Burdened by "guilt" they know that they must find the one solution to dissolve and dissipate that icy cold, silence. The responses to mollify the miffed from the guilt ridden are almost always the same: "What did I do wrong? Why won't you talk to me? Whatever it was that I did, I am truly sorry!"

Everyone who effectively uses the silent treatment on others is also a manipulator. Of course there are circumstances that happen in everyone's life where silence is truly golden. But it is also true that some people use silence to undermine or intimidate other people into doing whatever they want. The use of silence as a weapon, on the surface at least, appears to simply be a gentle but effective club that quietly forces the dominate will of one person onto the will of another person that only hopes to please.

The Submerged Goddess used silence against the Non Goddess because the Submerged Goddess was caught between two very powerful emotions: dislike and fear. The Submerged Goddess really disliked the Non Goddess but she feared being completely alone more. In a futile attempt to resurrect a part of her flagging ego, the Submerged Goddess required the Non Goddess to grovel and beg "forgiveness" for just being herself. The Submerged Goddess often employed the silent treatment against the Non Goddess and once the silent treatment ended the Submerged Goddess always managed to point out some insignificant flaw to the Non Goddess like the hint of a budding pimple or greasy hair each used as justification for the Submerged Goddess to be upset and cranky.

The Submerged Goddess often took offense that the Non Goddess didn't call as much as she thought she should to make plans for their weekend or maybe she didn't manage to make plans for the two of them to have a sleepover at the home of the Non Goddess. In this relationship with the Submerged Goddess the Non Goddess had to be the event planner, the initiator of all contact between the two. To fulfill her passive/ aggressive pedigree, the Submerged Goddess always complained about and was dissatisfied by any plans made by the Non Goddess. After living through three heart rending years, the frayed Non Goddess decided that her relationship with the Submerged Goddess was too painful and costly to maintain. The Submerged Goddess's power could be found in her ability to 'guilt' the Non Goddess into submission by making the Non Goddess feel wretched most of the time because she committed the sin of forgetting to call the Submerged Goddess or she hadn't managed to make plans for the weekend because she had other responsibilities.

The Submerged Goddess is a perfect role model for those who display passive/aggressive tendencies. The Non Goddess was completely unaware of the tactics used against her by the Submerged Goddess. The Non Goddess learned that her relationship with the Submerged Goddess caused her to experience many teary, gut wrenching nights that were filled with self-doubt and made her question whether or not she was even worthy enough to maintain a viable friendship with anyone, much less the Submerged Goddess. Conversely, the Submerged Goddess went to bed every night and slept peacefully without even a single thought about the Non Goddess and her needs. The sad truth is that the more distressed and out-of-kilter the Non Goddess felt, the better the Submerged Goddess felt. Of course this relationship had only one certain outcome. This relationship, just like other one sided or lopsided relationships don't stand the test of time. And as the months slipped by and turned into years the relationship between the two outcasts declined and devolved into something quite ugly.

As graduation day loomed for the Submerged Goddess and the Non Goddess, a miracle patiently waited in the wings for the Non Goddess. The Non Goddess applied to and was accepted by a prestigious private school. This meant that the Non Goddess would not attend the local public high school. When the Non Goddess informed the Submerged Goddess of her plan to attend a private school, the Submerged Goddess seethed with palpable jealousy and rage when she was informed about her 'friend's' good news. The summer after graduation brought the Non Goddess a surge in self-confidence while the Submerged Goddess began a concerted effort to expand her meanness against the Non Goddess which devolved into veiled attacks against the character and dreams of the Non Goddess. The Submerged Goddess methodically sharpened her attacks against the Non Goddess like a cat sharpens its nails on a scratching post.

The Submerged Goddess attacked in earnest. With every verbal insult and put- down flung by the Submerged Goddess, doubts began to loom in the pure heart of the Non Goddess. As her doubts increased and began to take hold the Non Goddess became uncertain and vulnerable and soon she lost touch with who she was and she began to question her dreams and aspirations and what she might become in the future. The poison filled words hit home with the Non Goddess because she was simply a thirteen year old girl without any sophistication. She was baffled by, what appeared to her as endless attacks, when all that she wanted was a best friend. Being betrayed by the Submerged Goddess became extremely significant to the Non Goddess because, like most adolescents, she needed to be accepted by her peers.

So, to try and explain why mean girls and male bullies manage to survive middle school and go on to high school to become master tormentors is based on the fact that most young people would rather be involved with peers who are mean and heartless rather than to be left alone and friendless. There is nothing more profound that can happen in a middle school student's life that defines them as a loser more so than being a loner without friends.

The worst that could happen to any non-goddess in middle school actually happened to a friend of mine. My friend was an obvious non-goddess although she was known throughout the entire school because of her sterling reputation as a good student and for being a sensitive human being. These attributes aren't respected by goddesses nor are these attributes normally practiced by the members of the popular groups in middle school. One day after classes had ended my friend was preparing to leave school as soon as her mother came to pick her up. While leisurely leaning against the building, this otherwise smart young lady mindlessly said "Hello" to the chief-resident-in-training goddess and popular group honcho. The word just kind of just slipped out of her mouth and in response, my friend reflexively flinched as she waited for the blast from the goddess. Instead, Ms Popular Goddess offhandedly returned my friend's "hello" in a breathy, exhausted sigh. This unexpected response, to say the least, shocked my friend. She told me that she felt like she had become suddenly airborne. Ms. Popular Goddess was obviously assured that she had an adoring audience and responded: "Oh Non-Goddess, you just don't know how lucky you are?" Engaged, the Non Goddess responded with an innocent: "Oh, really, why?" The Popular Goddess dramatically sucked in a deep breath as if she were taking a drag on a cigarette and then stared into the distance and said: "You just don't know how hard it is to be me…I mean, everyone expects me to be the most popular girl in school…So, be glad that you're," she pauses for effect..."just you!"   Now, if that isn't a classic goddess encounter, I don't know what is! It boggles the mind to think that this goddess-in-training had the nerve to be burdened by her own manufactured popularity.

You would think that adulthood and maturity would ensure that all grown-up girls would have learned how to avoid the goddesses. Yet, maturity and age don't always protect women from experiencing mean, back-stabbing behavior that marks most relationships ventured into with the goddess class. Little girls grow into women and women, like little girls, have always been vulnerable to the dewy eyed, almost always beautiful, arrogant, mean-spirited women in their lives. Middle school merely provides a platform for the germination of mean girls to grow-up and become full-fledged goddesses or adult mean girls. And many goddesses begin training as passive/aggressive little girls who learn how to use meanness and duplicity to further their personal agendas.

The good news is that middle school ends and the people that couldn't be avoided there leave and go to other places like high school and beyond. By the time students reach college, the non-budding goddesses feel certain that they have left all of these negative women and all of those pent-up feelings associated with never being quite good enough to be accepted into the popular group far behind them. What a shock it is to arrive at college and to be duped into trusting other passive/aggressive females who begin friendships like other normal, friendly human beings. And then after college women continue to meet and form relationships with women who are just as mean and unscrupulous as the mean girls in middle school. It is important to note that many people have passive/aggressive personalities. Every passive/aggressive female doesn't grow-up to become a goddess. Some little girls watch and 'feel' their mother's experience of suffering through being passive/aggressive and decide relatively early that all of that emotional pain isn't something they intend to experience in their lives. Many of these budding goddesses grow-up to torture their mothers and other people in their immediate family and their lives just to ensure that they will never feel the pain of fear like their mothers felt. The illness, like people, is complex. But being a goddess is not an illness, it is a choice!

And all goddess's have a big problem with not being able to be the center of attention all of the time. Some goddess mothers find it impossible to share the limelight even with their flesh and blood daughters. Some of these misguided goddesses actually think that it is acceptable to compete against their own daughters. It's a very sad day indeed to watch a full-grown woman compete with her daughter for the attention of her daughter's male friends. If a goddess is comfortable with competing for and taking away the attention of men and others from her own daughters, what could that tantamount of selfishness possibly mean for the rest of us?

Goddess Speak
Do As I Say, Not As I Do
Chapter 6

Daytime television talk shows over the last twenty years have spawned a new national identity for the American woman. Modern technology has transmitted this cultural phenomenon to women throughout the civilized world. This new powerful female identity has spread like wildfire in the United States and is the place where the world's most privileged women reside.

Today's modern American woman lives, literally, in the lap of luxury. American women have made gains both socially and economically largely because of the impact of the progressive, modern feminist movement that began in earnest again in the mid 1960's. The modern feminist movement was launched to not only provide American women with greater freedom and equality in the workplace but also at home as well. The 60's feminist movement also wanted to elevate and provide better lifestyles and opportunities to women. The recent feminist movement has largely succeeded in fulfilling its agenda because most American women not only expect equality in the workplace but American women, more than any other group of women on the face of the earth, have gained acceptance not only as line employees but as managers and CEO's as well.

On the vanguard of this feminist evolution, along with many unsung modern feminist, is Oprah Winfrey. Oprah has emblazoned the passions of the super feminist and the goddess class into the national consciousness of millions of American women. Oprah's show has also managed to gift many of her core audiences, meaning women, with a sense of entitlement that has never existed before. Although Ms. Winfrey is clearly responsible for shining that unblinking media eye on specific injustices against women and their children, she has also managed to side-step some of the real issues that still afflict many American women who never expect to weekly spa visits or to take their children on exotic vacations. Without a doubt, all women should be concerned with the mistreatment of other women whether that mistreatment falls into the realm of domestic violence, female genital mutilation and even deplorable and unacceptable living conditions. Ms. Winfrey is a current front runner in the daytime feminine talk show circuit and a feminine producer par excellence of female programming. Ms. Winfrey is also responsible for creating a new breed of Goddess/Divas who define themselves by their designer lifestyles rather than by their desire to change the ills that plague women in society.

In the shadow of Ms. Winfrey's empire, the progressive American feminist movement struggles to regain a foothold in the hearts and minds of many modern women who are more concerned with the bling-bling of modern life rather than dealing with the boring day to day details of making a difference in the lives of all women. The truth is that progressive American women have struggled for equality for centuries. In the past, early feminists came from the upper classes because these were the women who had the free time and the economic clout to be the arbiters of social justice. Poor women were and are either too busy or downtrodden to even dream of being able to make changes in their lives. These poor and downtrodden women have less than an even chance of changing the society that entraps them because they are largely invisible to the rest of society.

The so-called double standard where men are "more" equal than women in a society has been the major focal point of feminist movements in the past. Over the last forty years, American feminists have turned their attentions towards the workplace in an attempt to ensure true equality for both male and female employees. Unfortunately, for the common female working in the lower rungs of any profession, the issue of equal pay/compensation for performing the same job is a goal of the feminists that has yet to be realized. On average, in 2008, women earn seventy-seven cents for every dollar that a male earns.

The rise and entrenchment of the goddess class hasn't helped to spread a beacon of hope to the struggling American woman or impoverished women worldwide. In fact the rise of and the adoration of the goddess class by women has begun to tarnish the once bright glow of the feminist beacon that heralded a new day of equality for women.

Even though vestiges of the past double-standard between men and women still exists today in America ("Me Tarzan, you Jane!") the old canard is still being challenged and a new type of double-standard has arisen. The so-called new double standard has been embraced by the popular and the not-so-popular female talk show hosts and has been heartily embraced by goddesses across the American media landscape.

It's probably extremely unfair to lay the entire blame for this reversal in domestic tranquility in America at Oprah's feet, but Oprah and her band of experts are at the forefront of this new push for a re-hashed double-standard that has taken foothold between American men and women today. In order to understand the "new" double-standard, it will be necessary to investigate a series of life experiences from the past while comparing those experiences to current life styles.

For centuries, men and women have taken vows to love, honor, and whatever…one another for the rest of their natural lives; that is, if they decide to marry in the old-fashioned, traditional way. Most newly married couples experience the ups and downs that are simply a part of any union. Let's face it; living with another human being is just really difficult at times. In other words, learning to live with another human being can be a trying and difficult experience for most people. For women who grow up in a culture that embraces the idea that some little girls are fairy princesses in addition to embracing dream of growing up to be Cinderella dooms a lot of marriages. Both young and old newly weds discover that "love just doesn't conquer all." When that fever pitch glow of infatuation begins to cool between two people, living with another person can suddenly become unbearable. No one teaches us how to fall in love. Learning how to keep those love flames burning is probably one of the most trying jobs that most couples encounter. Most people fall madly in love and most walk into relationships, willingly and blindly, without the benefit of sage advice or instruction of any type.

Unless the female half of the union is already pregnant on that very special day, the wedding, then many couples choose to immortalize their gene pools by reproducing. Over the course of most marriages most couples co-habit, create progeny, and if their lucky, buy homes or start businesses. During this entire flurry of activity, both members of the union are also supposed to find ways to successfully further a career as well as find personal satisfaction. As the sands of time shift through a much defined hour glass for each of us, subtle things like that initial attraction or infatuation begin to ebb and wane as life and its cumulative hardships take their toll on the players. For the young, it is almost impossible to perceive a reality where breath-taking, heart pounding, knee-shaking infatuation could give way to complacent, predictable love where a once vivacious, sexually alluring, effusive young woman turned into dear old mom or where a tall, dark and dangerous young man turned into dear old, doddering dad.

With the passage of time in the lives of the newly hitched the gene of responsibility replaces passion and instantaneous physical titillation. Many married women begin to dream about and desire that illusive, tall stranger who instantly intuits her every unspoken desire and then acts to fulfill each one completely. The tall, dark, mysterious, and at times, brooding male is the meat of the popularity of female romance novels.

And men…well; all of you already know what you dream about and therefore it is unnecessary for me to explore your dreams here. Ah, if only that once sexually ardent female could once again lavish that keen interest and voracious need for me on a regular consistent basis, my life would be complete. Ah, if only!

But all is not lost. Although the texture of love changes as the rigors of responsibility overtake passion, the still vibrant couple begins to love one another in a different way where their love begins to encompass their responsibilities. And in their need to harness responsibility many couples sacrifice and lose their once all-consuming sexual spontaneity and their once overwhelming sexual prowess slips into obscurity. In most families the children become the wife's main focus in life and in that process her husband and his needs clearly fall behind the needs of their children whether his needs are real or imagined. The wife's basic orientation in life transforms her into making what she perceives to be the perfect family life for all of her family members. Most men are painfully aware that their once important role in the lives of their wives has shifted dramatically from key player to being a bench warmer. Caught up in their own disillusionment with their less than fulfilling lives, a few men notice that their wives are also living in an emotional and sexual wasteland. The bottom line is that many women like the men they are supposed to *share* their lives with, also feel alone and abandoned in a world that they are largely responsible for creating.

For most men, feeling neglected and being pushed to the sidelines of life by their wives and even by their once adoring children, many men become work-a-holics, avid golfers and a few stray to chase other skirts. The children learn to treat dear old dad in much the same way that dear old mom does; as an after thought. The shock for most men is that he was so easily replaced as the most important person in his beloved's heart. The constant rejection from his lady love begins to grate as his submerged needs begin to implode. His need naturally exacerbates his inability to fulfill his basic needs with the person he chose to spend the best years of his life. Many women emotionally discard the men they chose to marry not only for their children but often for their friends and/or family members. I like to call this female response to the mating conundrum the nesting quotient.

Many women treat their husband's as if they are an expensive pair of shoes that are worn infrequently. Almost all women have a special pair of shoes and since they are special this pair is infrequently pulled out of the closet or from under the bed for use on only rare and special occasions; just like their husbands. In other words, men like dress shoes are forgotten and put away on a shelf until needed. This typically is how the sands of time passes for an extraordinary number of couples and a great divide obviously begins to metastasize and eventually leads to mutual disillusionment and failed relationships. This slow drip of acid on the delicate tissues of love starts an almost irreversible path towards certain destruction. Life takes its toll on the lives of people who are supposed to be bound together forever because the principal players are clearly unaware of what it is that they need to feel fulfilled, happy and satisfied. And because most of these people are wholly unaware of what it takes to fulfill their own personal needs most are also totally unaware of what is necessary to fulfill the needs of the person standing right beside them in life; that person that they publicly committed to love, honor and…whatever.

Hence, tens of thousands of men and women wander through their lives feeling alone, underappreciated and frustrated. All because "love" is still one of the greatest highs that most people experience in their life times. This thing called love makes life worth living until that slow drip of acid and all those pesky "needs" conspire to loosen the love bonds. As the need to experience that special high, that all-consuming intensity of experiencing being in love, again, blots out common reality and turns into an unsatisfied hunger. The hunger peaks and as fate would have it, someone else is also equally in need of that special fix.

One bright and sunny day, or maybe it's "a dark and stormy night" when the neglected, abandoned and needy husband is almost forced to sniff around in search of what he can no longer expect to find at home. Now, please be aware that there are men who go on the hunt for sport and not out of neglect. The following is about neglected men with needs and possibly the mate of a goddess

The husband begins to notice that the world at large is full of desirable and beautiful women and more importantly; some of those women appear to be interested in…gulp….him. The attention starved man begins to notice the well-groomed (many wives, trophy wives and goddesses excluded allow their appearance to down grade after marriage and many more join the ranks of the under-groomed after childbirth) women who are either single or married and are still remarkably on the hunt. Most husbands enter the arena of infidelity innocently. The husband and his glaring needs are taken off-guard by a simple friendly "Hello" or maybe an arched eyebrow that signals appreciation from an open and friendly woman. Perhaps she also exhibits a perfect smile accompanied by an unmistakable whiff of a special scent gently wafting through the air as this attractive and friendly female passes.

In contrast, the husband's loving goddess is full of complaints and is almost always irritable and tired most of the time that he is at home. The crabby wife supplies her husband with an endless litany of complaints ranging from: "I have to do all the work around here!" to "These are your kids too…It would be nice if you'd manage to get home early once in a while so that I could get my nails and my hair done!" The once affectionate, long-ago sexually alluring woman has turned into a version of his mother - an asexual complainer that constantly treats him like an incompetent child who needs to have dandruff brushed from his shoulders to sighing deeply in displeasure in public at one of his jokes in front of his colleagues or friends. And the ultimate female insult to any man is to have his wife spit on a tissue and uses it to clean a spot or food from his chin, his cheek or tie in much the same way that she might clean something on one of their kids before meeting the grandparents or some other adult. For most men, all this mothering from the woman who used to light his jets and caused his juices to boil is simply too much of a giant step into a reality that most men would rather avoid. The one hint of remaining sexual desire and allure that the husband might expect from his once hot vixen might flash explosively after she finishes a somewhat steamy romance novel or, if he's truly lucky, on their anniversary or as a reward for some extravagant gift.

Is it any wonder that many men contemplate having sex with a stranger or maybe an acquaintance of two? Think about it. How many men approach their wives with the intent of engaging in sex play only to have that request rebuffed as if he had thrown a pebble into a glass surfaced lake with the ripples of his desire spreading towards the shoreline where the ripples just disappear into obscurity? Many married men become inured to their mate's sexual excuses that range from: "I have a headache," to "The kids are still awake," to simply "Don't touch me!" Many men simply stop trying to engage their mates sexually in an act that used to be the stuff of fantasies.

Most men and a whole lot of women are cursed with being all too human and many more have an active and alive libido. The husband, starved for affection becomes slavishly drawn to other women who are warm, open and friendly. Many of these "other" women exhibit a sense of humor and many appear to enjoy spending idle time just talking and laughing with a man whose wife only growls orders at him. The clincher is that most of these "other" women rarely, if ever, complain about anything. Not only are the women in the outside world warm and friendly but they also emit mysterious scents and always look good unlike their home-bound goddess who rarely dresses–up unless she is going to church or a PTA meeting. In time, the once innocent, casual relationship that began with a simple "Hello" leads to lunches and eventually a drink or two and dinner after work.

Needy and frustrated the husband allows the casual acquaintance to blossom into a full-fledged affair. As the illicit affair heats up, the wife-goddess begins to notice that her dependable and sex demanding husband has begun to dress himself with more attention to detail, wears a new after shave and that he also spends a lot more time grooming his nails and other physical attributes than he has in years. A few months may pass before the wife-goddess begins to realize that her husband's sex demands have declined or disappeared altogether and that his normal, annoying desire to spend time with her late into the evening has all but disappeared. As the husband becomes more involved and fascinated by a lively and sexually alluring female, his emotionally distant wife begins to feel uncertain as her woman's intuition kicks into high gear. Of course this secret can't remain a secret for very long. The wife-goddess starts to investigate her husband's new found contentment and the husband begins to leave tell tale signs of his affair in plain view for his wife-goddess to discover. The wife eventually puts all the pieces together and determines that her husband is having an affair and armed with this fact the wife makes sure that her husband's life shifts suddenly from a zone of clandestine peace and passion to a cauldron of hot boiling oil that can only be described as the punishing wrath of a betrayed woman.

After the discovery of an illicit affair, most goddess-wives respond quickly, swiftly and ruthlessly. Their wrath is generally unrelenting and exacting. Most husbands find themselves overwhelmed and submerged by their wives continuous bouts rage, anger and non-stop tears. Certain men are confused by their wife's swift and caustic response to their affair because these men can't understand how they, living as the invisible man all this time in "her" household, could suddenly morph into a person that actually caused his wife to feel something.

Most men start to "get it," that is, begin to understand the sense of betrayal that their goddess-wives feel once their lives become a living hell on earth spearheaded by a screaming and vengeful woman who has suddenly found time to verbally assault him, (that is if he's lucky because some women become physically violent) exclusively, while ignoring their children and her other duties. When not assaulting her cheating husband, the poor wounded dove spends most of her time pouring out her heart about her betrayal to her family, friends, neighbors or to anyone else who will listen.

During this phase of marital decline most intelligent men try to fade into the background if he still lives at the place he used to call home. Many men choose this time to either move-in with his mistress or, if he's smart, he tries to seek out some dark and shadowy corner (read cheap apartment or dingy motel room) that offers some sort of refuge from the non-stop vitriol from his beloved goddess, the woman of his dreams that has turned into the goddess of his nightmares. Some men choose to remain at home and pursue counseling, generally at the wife's request, in an attempt to patch up the badly broken relationship. Some men also end up reverting to childhood emotional responses that they developed as boys to deal with intense emotional or difficult situations. Most men caught in the middle of a goddess maelstrom of pain can only hope and pray to have the screaming along with the endless, tearful accusations and recriminations to cease quickly.

So many men, that is, the ones that still love their wives and kids and who also want to truly salvage what is left of their marriages will agree to almost anything that their goddesses demand. And most spurned wives require their philandering men to give them everything: that typically includes their dignity along with their balls on a platter. Most men, in the beginning stages of reconciliation will accept any and all conditions that the goddess sets forth. The cowed male will try as well to adhere to the extreme new terms in the relationship that translates into marital confinement expressed as: "You will make yourself available to me, by phone or by any other way I deem fit, whenever I request. You will also agree to be questioned endlessly on any issue regarding other women and you must answer truthfully, without hesitation about who you are with and what you are doing in order to satisfy and allay my suspicions!"

A lot of men step up to the plate and accept this childish punishment just to have their lives return to some semblance of order and normality. The sad fact is that no matter how much a cheating husband pleads for forgiveness from his scorned mate and no matter how much he subjugates himself to her insecurities; his actions will never fill the gaping hole left by his infidelity in his wife's heart and soul. What many people and especially scorned women fail to realize is that healing comes from within, much like forgiveness. In fact healing never begins until true forgiveness has been embraced by the harmed party.

Professionals who deal with marital indiscretions have come up with a series of activities for the male must do to receive absolution from their emotionally abused and betrayed goddess. Once upon a time, a long, long time ago, a simple heartfelt apology and a promise from the adulterer not to stray in the future was enough for most aggrieved wives. But that was a long, long time ago and like most things in our modern lives, a simple, sincere apology is not enough and especially so for the very well-paid professionals who treat the cuckolded goddesses.

Today, professional counselors, talk show hosts and women have decided that straying men can only expect forgiveness for committing that ultimate "sin" only by allowing his every thought, his every action and even his fantasies to be inspected and dissected by his spouse and each must be deemed non-threatening by his overly critical and unforgiving goddess or he will have hell to pay!

The roots of this so called marital tune-up or "treatment" for marriage reconciliations can be found in use in households all across America. After marriage, many goddesses begin to relate to their husbands much like they relate to their sons. Mothers and sons, just like husbands and wives, have always shared what can only be described as a love/hate relationship. Most mothers love their sons more than they love that next breath of life to fill their lungs although many mothers who have sons also hate not being able to completely control their sons' wild natures. Almost all American goddesses plan to change their 'dream guy' into the man of their dreams.

Men and women have historically approached life and how to solve life problems differently. These sometimes broad differences that exist between men and women and how they decide to problem-solve are considered by many to simply be personality quirks. Some women honestly believe that the Y, you know that it's missing a leg old saw, chromosome is wholly responsible for how men attack problems in completely different ways than women. Today's educated young women think that testosterone is the culprit that makes that eternal man-child (many, many women believe that men never grow-up) think and strive to do stupid and dangerous things. So, the process of living with men and seeing them do ridiculous things over the years has added an extra dimension to the divide that exists between men and women and how both genders decide how to accomplish things in their lives. Women grow up feeling and believing that they are "right" about most issues like how to raise a child or to how their husbands should manage career aspirations or how to drive the car.

Clearly, women are born with a genetic predisposition that allows them to feel that they know what is best for practically everyone in their lives. Maybe this female misperception begins at an early age like passive/aggressive behavior? Women, American women that is, simply "know" how men should live their lives and because most women are unable to influence and/or dictate behavior to their spouses all of the time, many women decide to exercise their innate desire to change how men think and respond to life early, by trying to break the willfulness of their sons. A woman's ability to comfortably nitpick at her son, and tangentially her husband, is a cornerstone of the love/hate that exists between mothers and sons and ultimately between husbands and wives. Many women are wholly unconscious of this demeaning habit because, to most women, their preoccupation with "rightness" is just how things should be; if only men would just stop and listen and then follow their advice, the world would be a much better place to live. To that end, there are very few goddesses who meet and fall in love with a man, even the man of their dreams, who doesn't believe that she can "mold" him into the man that she knows that he should become.

So, the current popular cure for most male adulterers would begin something like this from the viewpoint of a goddess:

1.) A simple heart-felt apology is never enough. (Whatever happened to "vengeance is mine saith the Lord!")
2.) He must cease all contact with the "other woman." (A reasonable request)
3.) He must be available and accessible to his wife 24/7. He will also be required to answer any and all questions about his whereabouts and who he is with. (Profoundly demeaning and dehumanizing at best)
4.) His current and future activities will always be suspicious. (Give me a break!)

5.) If he ever refuses to strictly comply with the foregoing, his refusal will be grounds for divorce and perpetual economic support. (What would happen if she was the adulterer? Without a doubt the steps to healing would be less restrictive and surely without economic recompense.)

The foregoing prescription that is supposed to help re-cement the pieces of a broken marriage is about as useful to a couple on the brink of divorce as recommending to a blind man that he get behind the wheel of any car and drive it on a crowded and busy freeway as fast as he can towards an exit five miles down the road. So, exactly why is the foregoing prescription to salvaging a failing marriage so bad?

To begin with, the formula negates the fact that the male adulterer is simply a flawed human being with needs and feelings that will surely respond negatively to the list of dehumanizing demands that are supposed to help his goddess to feel "secure" again. The truth is, security cannot be created by making an adulterous mate feel like he's been convicted of a heinous offense as if he were a serial killer/rapist and received a life sentence to be spent, without parole, in solitary confinement. Nor does real security exist in binding another person's being and needs to a series of demeaning activities in an attempt to assuage and remove the pain that often comes with infidelity. The hard truth is, whatever underlying reasons that were compelling enough to make it acceptable for a husband or wife to stray outside the marriage for sex or companionship are also the exact same reasons why demeaning demands will not yield a secure mate who feels better simply because the their partner apologizes or devotes their entire being to fulfilling the unrealistic demands of a hurt goddess.

The goddess class and far too many other women live in a haze of pop culture and a whole lot of denial when it comes to admitting and accepting that they are just as responsible for the decline of their marriages as are their cheating mates. When relationships fail it is solely because the two principals involved stop fulfilling each other's needs. When the dance of attraction and love begins between two people the dancers are completely unaware of the fact that each person is drawn to another person by unseen and often unacknowledged needs. When a relationship moves forward an unwritten and unspoken contract transpires between the two dancers and each partner is supposed to follow their part in the choreography of their dance to fulfill the conditions of the contract.

When trouble rears its ugly head during most marriages it is primarily because some major portion or maybe the entire unwritten contract has been violated or some key portions of the contract remains unfulfilled. For example: the age old unwritten contract between men and women is: "I'll have the children and I will also take care of our home as long as you provide a decent lifestyle for me." Another unwritten contract might be "When I was a child my parents never supported my dreams or aspirations. If we marry, you will always support me in my dreams and aspirations." Most unwritten contracts are established by people who are unaware that they personally have unacknowledged inner needs that they expect someone else to satisfy. The attraction that exists between people that leads to commitment and marriage is based on a kind of mutual chemical dance orchestrated by inner needs.

It's not necessary to re-state that living with other people is difficult. Just reach back through your personal sands of time and remember how many times you wanted to kill your brother or your sister or why you felt it was necessary to vacate your parent's home as soon as possible after you turned eighteen or maybe sooner. Normally, many young couples have slight disagreements before they decide to get married and most young couples are content with the idea that they will never experience anything more serious in their lives together than minor disagreements. The young couples who have major arguments before marriage should stop to closely examine what is causing the level of strife in their lives before taking another step towards life-long commitment. But all relationships have their ups and downs and most relationships have the resiliency to recover from the imagined or real slights that occur in all relationships. It is also important for all newly married couples to confront the possibility that an affair might take place in the future and to understand that is it possible for a marriage to fully recover after the devastating effects of an affair. The reason that these marriages survive the jolt of adultery is because the two people involved decide that both people need to work on their individual problems, first, before they can actually identify and correct the problems that exist between them in their marriage.

The disconnect that happens between couples and causes adultery basically occurs because both parties begin to turn away from one another and allow the minor annoyances of life to build-up and dominate their relationship. At the bottom of this disconnect between a husband and a wife is the fact that each party begins to feel betrayed on some personal level because some essential part of their unwritten contract isn't being fulfilled. Once hurt and disappointment begin to infiltrate the delicate tissues of commitment and love between two people, the irritation levels rise and the bile spews forth. Tension over unspoken slights naturally intensifies and mistrust sets in between the two people who until these problems arose, trembled in excitement whenever they were next to one another. The unreleased tension is the perfect breeding ground for the implacable wedge that pushes them farther apart.

For women, the most commonly revealed reason for that wedge and the eventual disconnect is the birth of children. As nurturers, women are supposed to turn all of their attentions towards preserving the lives of their offspring. Apparently women aren't as good at multi-tasking as they think they are and would have their men believe because once a woman steps up to the plate as the ultimate caregiver she also looses her ability to pursue, titillate and remain physically alluring and excited about that man who had a hand, so to speak, in helping her to bring those beautiful cherubs into the world. Many goddesses become super absorbed with their children to the exclusion of their mates. Of course there are hormonal and cultural reasons that women bond with their children to the exclusion of almost everything else in their lives except for the social ties that promote the well-being of those children. Regardless of the psychology or the pharmacology behind motherhood, it is also just as true that many goddesses use their children as an excuse to justify their inability or desire to cultivate and maintain healthy relationships with their husbands.

When a goddess's basic security is threatened by another woman, many women try to "guilt" their husbands into reconciling and staying in their relationship. The goddesses of the world enter into marriage to selfishly satisfy their not so hidden desires and many goddesses enter into marriage without an ounce of love or attraction for the man that they expect to give them the world. Of course some of these relationships work because certain men clearly want to establish a relationship with a trophy wife so that he can have trade-in rights down the road.

This type of female behavior is recognizable to both men and women and this type of unacceptable behavior is also tolerated by men and women alike. Most men in America are aware that to have a peaceful home life or to even expect to have a sexual tumble now and then with the wife, he had better accept and placate the demands of his goddess. The types of behavior modification that some men have to undergo to please their goddess ranges from benign to demanding. For example, a goddess might request her husband to attend church every Sunday with her; or the goddess might require her husband to purchase expensive jewelry for her; or that her husband arrange expensive and exotic trips to far away places; or to simply imply that he husband should buy her another luxury home. Many married goddesses have traditionally withheld sex from their husbands as an indication of their complete disapproval of her husband's behavior. Other goddesses choose to sulk and pout until their husbands are forced to apologize for their behavior just to be able to spend a peaceful night at home.

This might sound like a novel idea but women, like men, have the power to choose whether to be either happy or unhappy in their lives while many goddesses prefer to make their happiness dependent upon everyone else, that is, everyone except herself. Although only previously hinted at, goddesses have extramarital affairs just like men and often for the same reasons. Occasionally, goddesses can find it in their sweet little hearts to forgive other women for having affairs. But make no mistake about this type of forgiveness by a goddess; goddesses will condemn other woman for acts of infidelity as quickly as they might condemn a man. And for a very large group of goddesses, any man who strays for any reason is judged as a despicable dog! The only thing that you can be certain of is that most goddesses, if they ever have an affair, will find a way to justify and forgive themselves whereas few goddesses will ever fid it in their hearts to forgive their husbands for having an affair.

At some point, goddesses are going to have to accept the fact that they too have a responsibility to their mates and their relationships. The first thing any goddess should do before striking out to start a new relationship is to first understand who she is and what her needs are. Goddesses must step away from their long held fantasies about meeting and marrying some charming prince who is also inexplicable mixed with that joyous bad boy complex. Ladies, after sixties years of life, I can tell you that there aren't any knights in shining armor to come and whisk you off your feet and into the sunset to live with happily ever after. Adult goddesses must stop relying on their friends, television talk show hosts and so-called relationship gurus to define who or what is the ideal partner for them. Television shows like "Sex in the City" or romance novels are not the place to find critical information about your personal issues, no matter how entertaining. To at first try to find an appropriate mate and then try to build a life-long relationship with another human being deserves more than pop psychology, today, can offer.

Very few goddesses are honest with themselves about their real needs and desires because so many goddesses have learned to smile real pretty for the camera while pushing all those uncomfortable feelings, down and far away because the heroines in those novels are always whisked off of their feet by some strong, daring and dashing man who are all-knowing and all-giving. These gothic romance novel heroes manage to enter a relationship without emotional baggage. If only women, and men for that matter, could find ways to be brutally honest with themselves and with the other people in their lives, then maybe, just maybe people might begin to live more secure and fulfilling lives.

All relationships deserve to have participants who practice openness and truthfulness with one another which in turn fosters trust. And the idea that the first scintillating dash of mystery that happens between men and women are filled with excitement and ignition that lights that first blush of every new relationship, unfortunately recedes and dies after time. Unless you manage to be involved in serial relationships that end as the magic fades. As the sands of time passes effortlessly through the hour glass of our lives and changes into something new and different, so too do those active participants change into something different and exciting. As long as insecurities, misperceptions and fears are discarded along the way, most relationships can remain healthy and strong. If goddesses want meaningful relationships with men and other people, then goddesses must also be willing to invest as much of themselves as they demand from others.

Female Support Net Works
Yeah, Right!
Chapter 7

In the mid-1960's the Women's Liberation Movement arose from the ashes of the previous Progressive Feminist Movement that was launched in the early 1900's. The new feminist movement's focus began quite vocally and characterized the tenor and tone of future movements. Part of what made the revolutionary era sizzle with excitement was the groups of young people intent on making a change in the society they felt was designed to entrap them with useless and unnecessary social norms. The new Women's Liberation Movement first proclaimed that its concerns were also the concerns of the nation. The visual that came to symbolize the movement at the time was the picture of women burning their bras.

Women's groups organized and began to lobby for workplace equality for working women. A huge assumption was made at the time by both men and women about the future of women what with all of this banding together for a common cause: both groups assumed that women would basically change how they related to one another and ultimately how they related to men because of the movement's success in making changes in women's lives.

Let's expose the not-so-pretty truth about how women related to one another before the Women's Liberation Movement that began in the mid

1960's. Women had practiced "back-biting" and employed subterfuge against other women for eons and yet both men and women expected women to bond and replace these negatives habits with that new found sisterhood. The Women's Movement was supposed to have cemented honesty and openness between women as a foundation of their newly bonded relationship. In the past and today, feminine support networks were made-up of well-intentioned women who had sincere desires to help other women to achieve equality and to get a bigger piece of that fat American pie. The obvious gem of the idea sounds logical and doable, right? Well, in the emotional world of girls and women, the reality is... "well it is sort of doable, as in kind of."

If the feminists had truly banded together for the benefit of all American women, the goddess/diva class surely should have disappeared from the landscape all across America, right? Unfortunately for men and surely for the legions of non-goddess women in America, the Women's Liberation Movement did not free any us from the often cruel but typically mean shenanigans of the goddess/divas. In fact, forty plus years of improved and greatly expanded opportunities for women living in these United States hasn't diminished the legions of goddesses who mysteriously spring from obscurity and into our lives to plague us with their selfish and sordid social affairs. It would appear, just from perusing the front pages of magazines and watching modern, episodic, popular television that the bond of sisterhood hasn't turned all women into selfless, secure, and caring individuals. In fact, it appears that the opposite is truer than ever.

American society today is clearly filled with well-funded, and by design, visible goddesses. Just look at all the young media obsessed, self-absorbed women who neither have nor want any connection to the precepts of the women's liberation movement. Legions of young women today are more attracted to being a media "sex symbol" or the mistress of a very rich scion rather than earning her place in society by her own efforts. A whole host of today's young women are more interested in patterning their lives after goddesses like Paris Hilton/Nicole Ritchie or the diminutive and off-putting Jada Pinkett Smith rather than striving to be women of substance. Instead, far too many young women today prefer to immerse their senses and their days with a media saturated with selfish and rich personalities they'd love to imitate like the brats on

"My Super Sweet Sixteen" or the obnoxious young women who go out of their way to be completely unpleasant and antagonistic on "Bridezillas." "Bridezillas" manages to expose young women with serious character flaws who are clearly unsuited for marriage or any other type of long-lasting relationship because the only thing that seems to bring these divas joy is for them to insult the group of sycophants who endure their insults with smiles. Isn't it all too clear that the goddesses are enjoying their new found, important status as media darlings while non-goddesses wonder where all this display of inane selfishness will ultimately end and more importantly, why has this type of, over-the-top aberrant behavior become a national pastime and accepted fad as popular culture in the first place?

On the other side of the coin is the vanguard of the Women's Liberation Movement who wanted all American women to embrace its philosophy and to unite in sisterhood. The design of the feminist movement and the its goals in the recent past was a flawless and doable concept but sometimes putting a flawless concept into a consumable and realizable form for the masses doesn't always materialize in the current reality of everyday people.

Countless young women can recount their own personal horror stories about the awful girls that they attended middle school, high school or the pain and misery that their college dorm mates gave them. These young ladies sojourn through life can be compared to the lives of other non-goddesses and each had to persevere regardless of the effects of their goddess tormentors along the way. Some college roommate goddesses decide that they have to ruin the personal and academic lives of a roommate or other female students simply because they could. These dorm room goddesses were supposed to have been a part of the advanced and enlightened sisterhood of women that knew that they were supposed to support one another. Yet the reality of the support offered by goddesses to their non-goddess "sisters," is often less than supportive and is generally quite a bit more vindictive and motivated by deception and hatred rather than sisterhood.

I appreciate the fact that I had the opportunity to attend college unlike a lot of women. College attendance for women in the past as well as today is for the most part for students who are fortunate enough to be able to afford to attend full-time classes. For many students college can also be a haven away from over-protective and/or demanding parents. College is also supposed to be a place where young people can finally find what it is they'd like to do with their lives and in that process figure out "who" they are. For another type of student, going away to college is the place where cheap beer is accompanied by alcohol-laced, transient sexual encounters, flowing freely and often.

Unlike some college students I attended only a few parties. Truthfully, I didn't lead the typical college student's life of dancing the light fantastic. You see, I felt that I owed my parents. "OMG! Was that a sign of maturity peeking out from the recesses of my youth?" And more importantly, I knew that I also owed myself the opportunity to do my very best that I could in school. Besides, learning new things had always been an exciting adventure to me.

My sophomore year in college presented me with all kinds of challenges, not just the roommate kind. The roommate goddess who had crossed my path also decided to create a ruse for my betterment which was largely predicated on her pretending that she and I were the best of friends. After dealing with several passive/aggressive 'friends' in middle school I was naturally a bit wary of this "new" friend who had been a rather passive/aggressive roommate. My roommie constantly talked about her allegiance to feminist issues and her firm belief in sisterhood. It took quite a few years for me to reconcile what had happened in this relationship that was supposed to be based upon feminist principles. Although most of the words that poured from her mouth were cloaked in feminist ideology, her actions mimicked those of the mean girls that I had encountered in middle school and high school. The point is, unless I thoroughly misunderstood the concepts of sisterhood, this goddess clearly never believed in sisterhood. The Pixie Goddess decided that I was her new pet project to unpack, in other words, to destroy. My roommate had become the personification of that new sisterhood of the modern feminist culture, that is, the goddess culture that thrives on discarding people in their lives without even an emotional ripple. It's as if these goddesses were replacing the people in their lives as if they were buying a new pair of jeans or shoes .to replace the old ones.

Here is a short preview of how the new sisterhood works. As fate would have it, I ended up in a few classes with people who were in the goddess clan with my roommate, the Pixie Goddess. Unfortunately it became common knowledge that I was also a stellar student and that useful piece of information helped the sisterhood to launch a campaign to help me to become a better person by helping me to end my addiction to being an academic nerd. The campaign began when I received an unexpected and unexplained visit from different 'friends' of the Pixie Goddess in places that I was known to study like the library or the parlor in our dorm late at night.

The sisterhood of college goddesses began their singular, ah, what shall I call it, intervention rescue therapy for me quite subtly. One of my classes was particularly difficult because the students were required to read a thousand pages weekly and in order to ace the class, four scholarly research papers had to be well-researched and well-written. The rigor of this class forced many high achieving students into the realm of being floundering students, each who would have been grateful to have eked by with a passing grade.

Remarkably, a lone student blew the curve for the rest of the class by scoring a ninety-seven on an extensive essay exam. With fate always playing an active part in my life, I was the student who blew the curve. Since I blew the curve for the entire class and the professor inadvertently revealed my identity to another student in my class, it wasn't too long before the entire class knew who had received the top grade. Instead of my fellow students congratulating me I became the class pariah because students tend to also be human and all human beings feel more comfortable if someone else is suffering right along with them. Apparently the news reached and so offended the Pixie Goddess that she and her toady friend who was also in my class decided that it was high time that I become the object of their sisterly personal make-over.

My fellow classmates mentally regrouped after the initial shock of just how much they were going to have to step-up their game to get a good grade in that class and their anger finally began to wane as new material changed the landscape of the class. No matter to the Pixie Goddess and her toady goddess friend. They both just fumed. At the time, I never realized how powerful that a spurned fellow classmate's ire coupled with the vindictive notions of a goddess roommate combined could explode from the dark recesses of academic competition into a kind of competition that I had never dreamed existed. The previous not so subtle, benign attacks from the Pixie Goddess and her troupe of goddesses had sufficiently crippled my self esteem. But the worst of their venom was yet to be unleashed.

One afternoon, a few weeks after the grade incident, the Pixie Goddess and her, let's call her Crony Goddess were lounging together in our room while discussing how they could each be more supportive of other female students. What a crock!

Okay, I'm exaggerating. I'm not psychic and my crystal ball that day was actually a bit foggy but the real truth is I really don't know what the two of them were talking about before I entered the room. I had managed, in between classes and work, to rush back to the dorm room for a quick change of clothes. My entrance into our room apparently struck the Pixie and Crony Goddesses dumb. I was initially greeted by the two of them with a stony silence enhanced only by the kind of chill that seeps into your bones on a very cold day. My instincts should have gone on full alert because the hairs on the back of my neck had stood up again in warning. Time seemed to have stopped and become frozen. The tableau changed ever so slightly as the two goddesses shifted their positions on the bed as they agreed silently to greet me (an act that was completely out of context) with large, toothy, disingenuous smiles. Pixie Goddess managed to croak out: "How are you and what are you doing here so early? Don't you have work?"

I think it would be kind of you at this point if you simply decided that I'm a social idiot. For whatever stupid and unexplainable reason I blithely ignored the hair on the back of my neck was by now waving vigorously to alert me to all the past humiliations and pain that I had endured because of these two mean-spirited goddesses

After their sugary "Hellos," what seemed like an eternity passed before the Pixie Goddess verbally oozed towards me and dripped: "Do you have a minute?" Again, I must admit that I made a series of stupid moves that day. Maybe I just couldn't or maybe I just wouldn't grasp the fact that there really are just mean women in the world who go out of their way to undermine other women. Maybe I'm just an eternal optimist. Maybe I was just plain lonely and I wanted to try one last time to smooth out the rough, really jagged edges of our non-existent relationship as I flailed emotionally trying to quell those flaming coals that represented the semblance of our relationship.

So, my desire to clear the air and to make "nice" outweighed my inborn instincts to run like hell. So, I willingly sat down and waited to see what the Pixie and Crony Goddesses had to say. Oddly, I felt like I was a mouse trapped by a cat and it was clear to me that the cat wasn't interested in eating me just yet. The Pixie Goddess was extremely calm, her voice steady. Crony Goddess was fidgeting. The conversation began innocently enough. "So, how's it going…I mean like how's things with you and your boyfriend?" She paused, although she was not really waiting for a response. "How are your classes going?" Dread began to creep up my spine. I was stunned because the Pixie Goddess hadn't inquired about my well-being for quite a while. I guess the hairs on the back of my neck began to suffer from stress tension because they laid down. The traitors! I began to relax a bit until Crony Goddess found her voice and spat out: "So how are things going for you in our class?" Without thinking and without having the emotional dexterity to even begin to suspect guile I responded: "Good! Things are good!"

The Crony Goddess leaned in towards me and the sickly sweet smell of her lipstick made the contents in my stomach jolt. Crony Goddess's eyes were shooting darts at me and her rate of breathing in and out increased dramatically. Crony Goddess was leaning so close to my face that I could almost feel the air escaping from her nostrils as it flowed rapidly in and out of her nose. It quickly became clear that Crony Goddess was furious. It became impossible for her, at this point, to control the volume of her voice so she chose to whisper: "So, ah…ah…do you know who scored the 97 on that last exam?" The question and her constant fidgeting affected me and caused me to fidget as well as the reality of what she knew began to dawn on me. Thankfully, she was on a roll and she wasn't waiting for any responses from me: "Well, I know…. And so does everybody else in our class." Then the Crony Goddess stood up and began to pace about like a caged animal in the small space that was our dorm room. She stopped abruptly in mid-pace. She tried desperately to regain control of her anger as she sat, dramatically, directly across from me. Her face was flushed and beads of sweat dotted the top of her lip and nose. She hurled words at me as if she was spitting out a very bitter lemon: "It was you and don't try to deny it!" Her venom was so potent that I physically shrank back from her and I immediately began to feel guilty about the grade and I almost allowed myself to feel dirty because I realized that I had betrayed her and all the other students in my class.

My emotional response to her emotional and verbal attack happened because good ole Crony Goddess had managed to strike some very deep emotional scars from my past. That act of exposing my prior, vulnerable emotional pain flung me back to a time when my mother had only to look at me with consternation or dissatisfaction which in turn made me respond first with compliance and then shame. And God help me if my mother was ever angry enough with me to actually voice that dissatisfaction; I'd locked myself away in the bathroom for hours.

And therein lays the full power that many goddesses use against other women. Goddesses, like most mothers, know how to make their children quickly snap to and out of negative behaviors. The kids of course, if in public or with friends, try to brush aside their obvious brush with death by pretending to willingly toe the line without fear. Goddesses like moms know how to emotionally inflict pain, uncertainty, or guilt in other women. The one emotion that almost all women try to avoid is the one that makes them feel humiliation. And the goddesses-in-training in middle schools across the land learn how to effectively flex that emotional muscle against others. That muscle that is perfected for use over time almost always hits its mark as the targets squirm and the mean girls bask in emotional euphoria. Mean girls in middle school learn how to brow-beat and humiliate others as easily as kittens learn to catch small prey and bat them about from paw to paw until the poor thing dies of fear or exhaustion.

Even though this was college and not middle school the experience with Crony Goddess left me feeling guilty and humiliated just because I had been a stellar student. I have to say, that this particular encounter has to be one of the hallmarks of sisterhood for me personally, something for me to look back on in my waning years with wonder and disbelief. But the guilt that I felt that day wasn't enough for the goddess sisterhood. They each wanted and needed to extract a pound of flesh from my hide.

Apparently, Crony Goddess had just begun her attack and since she felt my obvious emotional recoil she gained confidence to plunge on. The air in the dorm room became electrically charged as tiny sparks of electricity flecked and fizzled on the carpet between us as she moved from the carpet to blanketed bed. The natural light in the room seemed to dim as the storm clouds descended over her face. The Pixie Goddess began to pace briefly as well as the two suddenly launched a renewed assault against me. It began by them trying to undermine my emotional stability. Pixie Goddess led with: "You know...you really do need help. Professional help!" My stomach clinched and became the site for a not so perfect storm considering that I am prone to IBS when I'm under stress. Most women are extremely uncomfortable with confrontation and I am certainly no exception to the norm. All of my life I have tried to avoid confrontation and to make matters worse, this out in the open bit of confrontation was what the Pixie Goddess's had wanted for months, a direct, in your face confrontation. Since I grew up in a household where my family expressed themselves verbally and usually quite loudly, I finally began to recognize the earmarks of a mega confrontation.

The Pixie Goddess looked conspiratorially at the Crony Goddess as she hurled these sisterly (please understand the irony here) words of advice: "Don't you understand that being an overachiever is harmful? You need to chill out." Satisfied, she managed to pause as she dramatically sucked in her pixie breath. "I'll gladly recommend you to my therapist. After a few sessions, we'll hang out, just you and I. And once you get the hang of being healthy," pausing again dramatically, "like us, you can start hanging out with my girls on the weekends. Now wouldn't that be awesome?"

My stunned silence caused the storms clouds in the room to coalesce. I decided that it was high time for me to change my clothes and to get my ass out of that room as quickly as possible. I knew that a quick exit on my part was the only answer because I had suddenly become aware of just how ridiculous this whole thing had become. I had to get out of there quickly because I was about to uncork and laugh right in their faces. Of course I was stunned by their flaky ruse of supposed sisterhood shrouded in what they considered their incredible exhibition of caring selflessness evidenced by their foregoing sisterly pep talk. I mean, all you have to do is to consider the facts: 1). the goddesses united to help me cope with and change an obvious problem; academic over-achievement; and 2). they both offered me 'help' for my problem; which to them meant counseling with a therapist who regularly provided them with happy pills; and 3). the all timer, the goddesses were going to let me hang out with them! I could be the proud recipient of their selfless sisterly acts of love and inclusion if I just learned how not to be an overachiever. It was almost too much for me not to drop a tear from my misty eyes once I clearly understood their selfless offer of sincere friendship. How could I refuse their selfless offer to improve my social status and join their closed and powerful group at the price giving up a chance at a stellar education? After thoroughly evaluating and considering their offer, for a brief a second or two, I managed to shake my head "no" and bolted from the room before the giggles bubbled up and burst from the depths of my chest.

To be truthful, I had never heard of two people before who had the gall to suggest to a third party that they needed psychological help because they managed to maintain a near perfect GPA. Well, as crazy as it sounds, these two goddesses along with a select group of other students were disturbed by my dogged determination to be an avid student at the expense of having a social life. The worst thing about this scenario lies in the fact that there are women who will trample on the dreams of other women despite the fact that all women are supposed to be united in "sisterhood." Women are supposed to embrace and practice sisterhood. In other words women are supposed to support, cheer on and mentor other women. But of course the goddess culture misses what sisterhood is all about because most goddesses are actually selfish piranhas. I used to think that the Pixie and Crony Goddesses were immature and misguided and that by insisting that I seek therapy for a non-malady was a sure sign that these two women desperately needed contact with the real world and how real people are supposed to get along with one another. Once again my personal instruction kit was in a growth mode about how women really treat one another evolved and reflected some of the ugliness that some women use to pollute the environment for the rest of us.

The truth is that feminists actually have real and extremely important issues that they should be working tirelessly for on behalf of all women. Instead, the goddesses of the movement have decided that they would rather censure the choices and actions of other women rather than tackle the real issues that impact negatively on all women's lives. Take for example the feminist attitude that arose towards Hillary Clinton after it was revealed that Bill Clinton was a womanizer and an adulterer. A ton of feminist support for Hillary all but dried up after Hillary stated, publicly, that she chose to remain in a relationship with her husband.

Today, as a front-runner in the race to be the first female United States president, Hillary Clinton has regained the support of many feminists. But in the recent past, Hillary has been slandered and rebuffed by prominent goddesses as their tongues wagged and labeled her a traitor to their cause because Hillary chose to remain with her husband. I'd like to know when and why it has become necessary for certain goddesses to demand that other women make life altering changes and choices that are inconsistent with their needs, beliefs or desires. Apparently, the feminist movement has evolved and embraced a male attitude wherein "certain goddesses" know better about certain issues than the woman who's attempting to live her life on her own terms.

Gloria Allred, a well-known feminist attorney, is on the forefront of many legal cases that typically involve women whose legal problems have thrust them into instant notoriety in the media. Ms Allred typically wears red power suits made famous by Republican goddesses of the late 1980's and has surely garnered and surpassed her fifteen minutes of fame. Allred and Nancy Grace of CNN fame are both attorneys and both have exhibited on national television that they are more concerned with being blood sucking media hogs than really being concerned about the women that they claim to defend. These are two glaring examples of feminism gone wild!

Elizabeth Vargas is a prominent national newscaster who stated a few years ago that she was going to leave her post as a television anchor because she simply wanted to take time off to be a full-time mom. The outrage from feminists across the country who were against her decision was appalling and definitely not sisterly because these women, claiming to be feminists, demanded that Vargas simply dismiss her personal desires and maintain her high-profile job for the sake of the movement rather than taking a stand to show support for Ms. Vargas's desire to be a stay-at-home mom. Why do modern feminists believe that they have the right to tell other women to give up their personal desires in order to embrace the ideals of an organization?

The goddesses of the feminist movement have evolved from a group of women bound by a common desire to create avenues that make life better for all women to a group of harpies who are intent on controlling the lives of other women much like the men they so vehemently spurn. The feminist movement today prefers telling other women what to do or what to wear rather than fighting for and against real issues like universal affordable health care or living wages for all employed women, especially those women who are trapped at the bottom rung of the work force who are so typically the head of single family households with young children.

Where are the feminists when millions of women and their children go to bed hungry at night? Where is the feminist support network for the women whose lives have fallen apart and are forced to live on the streets or in shelters? Where are the feminists when young girls begin to shape their bodies to resemble the emaciated young models prominently displayed on the covers of national fashion magazines or on those coveted catwalks? Where are the feminists when young, typically beautiful women offer themselves on the pages of upscale magazines to wealthy, powerful old men?

The list of important issues that the sisterhood of feminists should be interested in the interest of all women is of course quite a long one. The point is that the modern goddess feminist rarely think about spearheading projects that have real value to the common woman because the goddesses see themselves and their pet issues as being more important than real life issues that affect the lives of millions of women. Peering in from the outside, it would appear that feminists today are only interested in spearheading fluff projects and controlling other women's lives by telling them how to dress, what to think, and how to live. And therein lays the great conundrum in the foundation of modern day feminists: modern feminists seek power to control and not to free other women from domination by other feminists. Despite the fact that this modern feminist movement boasts prominent members of all races, the movement is still largely exclusive and not inclusive of all women from all walks of life. The exclusivity of the group can be traced to the numbers of working poor women who have prominent positions within the organization, poor women with a voice that can sway the focus of the organization to address the glaring needs of this particular group of women. As expected, the numbers of visible, powerful, poor feminists are abysmally low. Until the vanguard of the feminist movement recognizes that the there are millions of women without a voice and begins to incorporate the needs of these women into an active and inclusive organization, then the sisterhood movement will continue to be fragmented by goddesses who will continue to run the organization like a high school clique. The sad fact is that there are a host of women who recognize that the feminist movement represents just another yoke to be placed around her neck rather than as source of hope and help.

In every woman's lifetime, that is if she is fortunate, she'll have a best girlfriend. Well once upon a time I had someone that I considered to be my best friend. She was moderately tall and she sported one of those slight figures with no real breasts or hips to write home to mom about. The color of her eyes, face and hair coupled with her openness about sex seemed to be the electrifying ingredient that made men swoon. She also had brilliant and perfect white teeth.

My best girlfriend and her future husband were responsible for introducing me to my future husband therefore I should be appropriately grateful to them both. But fate once again enters my life and expanded my understanding of the goddess class. Although the four of us bonded in a weird sort of way it was difficult to peg because we had absolutely nothing in common. Maybe we individually felt the need to hang out with one another in a safe relationship; therefore we forged a relationship based on social niceties rather than substance. Even my "to be" husband shared little to nothing with her "to be" husband yet we found ourselves spending time together at drive-in movies and over night-parties at their apartment. Because both of our "to be" husbands were in the military, she and I spent a great deal of time in her car at their Marine Corps base.

One thing became quickly clear about my so-called best friend; she was quite fond of sharing herself, literally, with her future husband's military friends. I became aware of her habit after my "to be" husband proposed marriage to me. Apparently my best friend was consumed by an overactive libido and she had no problem satisfying her insatiable need for sex with her husband's 'friends.'

Since she and I were best friends at the time, most of our conversation revolved around my enchantment with my projected future mate. After a very few dates, I just "knew" that he was the man that I was going to marry. Being best friends with, let's call her, the Snake Goddess, I had no problem confiding all of my feelings and misgivings to her about who I thought I was going to marry.

I don't know why everything occurs on bright and sunny days in my life but this particular day really was bright and sunny. My friend and I drove down to the Marine Corps base to pick up our guys for the weekend. Goddess Snake in the Grass and I were sitting in her car across the street from their barracks. And then this incredible looking guy stepped out on the second floor deck of the barracks wearing a pair of aviator sun glasses enhanced by his golden brown tan and of course that starched and tan military uniform. This guy was the most incredible looking male specimen that I had ever laid eyes on. I wasted no time in telling Goddess Snake in the Grass: "Oh my God! He is so hot!" The Snake Goddess slowly swiveled her head in my direction and then turned fully towards me and stared incredulously. After a beat or two, she explained just who the hot guy was as he languidly crossed the street and headed towards the car. I almost couldn't contain my excitement as the words fell lightly from her perfect lips: "That's your boyfriend, you idiot!"

Luckily, I was able to compose myself before he arrived at my side of the car. Composed outwardly and a quivering mess inwardly, the man of my dreams bent down slightly to kiss me gently. As he stood up he flashed a brilliant white smile and the smell of him permeated every cell of my body. He opened the car door, reached for my hand and gently pulled me towards him for a full body hug. It was everything I could do to maintain my composure and not have my knees buckle under me. I had dated quite a lot before I met this guy, yet I knew instantly that he was the "one." Oh, I had been attracted to others but no one had ever made nervous in the way he made me nervous. With all the other guys, I had always been in control. With this lean, mean Marine, I was completely out of control. My knees shook as I struggled to make my legs move towards the back passenger door so that he and I could slide into the backseat. He literally took my breath away. His scent filled my nostrils was completely intoxicating and that slight, confident smile that played around the corners of his mouth only made me more nervous. I tried to breathe in deeply to slow my racing heart but my head began to feel like it was a giant, inflated balloon. The silence between the two us was filled with our unspoken feelings that flitted between us like two magnificent butterflies. I was content to sit, silently, in the backseat with his hand lightly placed on top of mine as we waited for the Snake Goddess's fiancé to join us.

We left the base and returned to my friend's apartment located in central Los Angeles. Too many years have passed since that day and I can only remember the things that either made my heart skip a beat or slowed it down to a crawl. The evening passed uneventfully. The Snake Goddess and I were supposed to be doing the dinner dishes, together, but in actuality I was the only one doing the work as she sat and painted her nails. I somehow missed that she wasn't really paying attention to me. I was too caught up in a magical fantasy world filled with the man of my dreams and all the possibilities that could take shape. Turning away from the task at hand and towards my friend, I said words the that I considered to be the most important words that I would ever say in my lifetime: "I'm going to marry him!" The Snake Goddess adjusted her slim frame on the chair and stopped blowing on her wet nails, but only briefly. She paused dramatically and looked at me with rye amusement and snorted out: "He'll marry me before he'd ever think about marrying you." Being naïve or perhaps being simply stupid, I never even considered that she was serious. I thought that she was kidding because her wedding was just a few short week away. She enjoyed a private, personal giggle, a joke that I had completely missed, and returned to finish her nails.

A few days later my Dream Marine came to visit me at my home. He had made arrangements to stay at the apartment with his Marine buddy and the Snake Goddess. The two guys had arrived at the apartment around two in the morning. My Dream Marine decided to sleep on the living room floor in a sleeping bag because he was totally exhausted after a week of playing war games. Sound asleep for an hour or two; my Dream Marine woke up to take a pee. Groggy and disoriented, he flung the sleeping bag aside as he tried to adjust his eyes to the surrounding dimness. He hesitated again before getting up and on the way up, to his utter amazement, stood the Snake Goddess straddling his head in a black negligee and a smile.

The Snake Goddess smiled invitingly down at him and asked: "See anything you want?" Being an honorable man and friend my Dream Marine whispered: "No! There's nothing there for me to want." The still silence was shattered by the Snake Goddess stomping off to her bedroom and slamming her bedroom door.

This is the kind of wanton, cold betrayal that often happens between so-called female friends. This is another one of those sisterhood rituals that occurs between women all too often. How many times have you heard of someone's best friend or even a blood relative like a sister or a cousin having sex their boyfriend, or worse, their husband? Everybody has heard at least one horror story about someone being betrayed by another woman that she thought that she could trust. All too often many women consider themselves to be card carrying feminist and yet many of them managed to discard loyalty and trust between sisters just for a romp in the hay with a tantalizing male that is off-limits.

The thing about modern day sisterhood is that the feminist movement has become a movement for "some" women and the rules don't apply to everyone. The cadres of women who protest the loudest about women's rights are also the first to exclude other women from their ranks based on whether prospective sisters fit into their social class, their economic tier, or attended the same tony college or were members of the same sorority, ad infinitum. The point is, grown up women are not much different from those middle school mean girls who managed to create those loathsome cliques that made it A-okay to exclude others. In fact, the sad truth is that grown-up girls are just better at that age old game of exclusion and being mean.

Domestic and Social Tranquility
Chapter 8

Many women are known for possessing a unique ability to inflict emotional pain on others just by their verbal expression. Many men have learned to reflexively flinch from the sharp tongues of their wives, mothers and female bosses because of this "talent." Some men aren't emotionally equipped to be able to shrug off a verbal assault from a woman. Therefore, far too many emotionally ill-equipped men simply "lose it" whenever the women in their lives begin to verbally hammer on them about their flaws or some other personal failing. The following is in no way offered as a defense of any man who ruthlessly pummels the woman in his life to either elicit control or compliance or to merely exact silence from her because he can't stand to hear the sound of her voice for one more second. But the sad fact remains that many of the men who resort to physical violence against a woman does so to offset some inner frustration that may have been initiated by a woman's verbal taunting that in turn made him feel emasculated and/or worthless.

A disturbing change is affecting society in America today. The social landscape in today's American society is overrun by insulting young women who feel that they are privileged and above recrimination for their often rude and clearly antisocial behaviors. Many women in America suffer from an extreme sense of entitlement and many young American women feel that they have the right to verbally assault total strangers or acquaintances s simply because these darlings have had a bad day or feel the need to sharpen their claws on someone's hide.

Most of these modern social misfits are confirmed and confused goddesses. These goddesses quickly become contentious if they feel that their fleeting desires are being thwarted. The goddesses appear to physically expand in public especially when they feel justified in unleashing their brand of verbal insult against a complete stranger. Often, the subject of a public attack is generally male because the goddess feels inherently safe to insult and demean a civilized man in a public place without fear of repercussions, either verbal or physical. This theory becomes an interesting social phenomenon when this type of anti-social behavior occurs, often in civilized places like up-scale shopping malls or grocery store parking lots or at the few dog parks.

It's interesting because the goddess class carefully chooses their prey and most goddesses manage to confront others only in environments where the goddess feels especially safe. Very few goddesses have committed a socially stupid act wherein her verbal attack a poor and/or desperate man in a questionable neighborhood might put her in physical danger. Goddesses truly enjoy flexing their privileged muscles against others whenever and wherever their sensibilities have been disturbed by someone they consider annoying, offensive or beneath their stature.

Unless you are glued to your computer chair it is very easy to experience this now common, natural phenomenon of encountering the angry goddess almost anywhere in the United States. Goddesses are known to spend a lot of time updating their wardrobes or going to the spa for a massage to relieve all of that pent-up stress from their oh-so-busy lives that naturally accumulates in their fragile, rail thin bodies. No one know how difficult it is to cope with the pressures of shopping to maintain a chic, designer image. During most weekdays in the early afternoon hours most malls have an abundance of available parking spaces and most of these available spaces are miraculously near mall entrances. Even in this deserted hunting environment, the goddess class seems to lay claim to privilege.

It's a typical Wednesday or Thursday on a mild wintry day in southern California which means the temperature is a mild 68 degrees. That particular day the parking lot in front of Nordstrom's Department Store resembles a deserted drive-in theatre. Less than fifty cars dot the lot. Five cars pull into the same entrance at the exact time and into the same lane. It seems as if every driver has decided, unconsciously to park in the same place at the same time. The five cars were queued, one behind the other, waiting for the front car to park in a space that was soon to be vacated; or so everyone assumed.

It quickly became clear that the person that was in the coveted space wasn't as ready to leave even though the back-up lights on the vehicle were clearly visible to each of the five queued cars. Literally two minutes passed before the first car decided to drive away and look for another parking space. As the clock ticked and the person in the space continued to sit in their car, the line of cars decreased, left one by one as everyone decided to find an alternate space in which to park. The once coveted prime parking spot was still oddly occupied by the same car that was there when everyone arrived simultaneously, their back-up lights screaming to the rest of us: "I'm leaving now!" A well-groomed young woman probably in her mid-thirties to early forties peered into her rear view mirror. The goddess was well-groomed, blond and apparently stuck in that spot. Once the blonde goddess determined that all of the cars in the queue had parked elsewhere, she finally decided that she could finally leave the coveted spot.

The bizarre tableau unfolded before our very eyes because I had the pleasure of being in one of the queued cars, waiting patiently with a dear friend. My friend and I also abandoned all hope of parking the primo spot and found another spot that would have been coveted by the Queen of England on a busy Saturday afternoon. After we parked, my friend's curiosity had been piqued by the actions of the Blonde Goddess. My friend is one of those women who is a humanitarian, first, and as such she was concerned about the Blond Goddess's well-being. She began to wonder out-loud whether or not the Blond Goddess was experiencing some sort of mechanical problem or even a medical emergency. At the very least, thought my altruistic friend, the Blond Goddess might have been involved in a very important cell phone business call. A sense of relief crossed my friend's face once she realized that the Blonde Goddess had miraculously managed to vacate the coveted spot and that she didn't appear to be in need of medical attention or the assistance of a tow truck company.

Once my friend ascertained that the Blonde Goddess was okay and that her brand new Lexus SUV wasn't be suffering from mechanical problems, we decided to head into Nordstrom. As my friend and I approached the entrance to Nordstrom's, we turned towards the sound of a honking horn, as in a warning of impending danger. My friend and I looked up and from side to side quickly to ensure that our lives weren't in peril. To our surprise, the now in motion Blonde Goddess slowed down in her gleaming Lexus SUV, lowered her car window and flashed us a bright and cheery smile accompanied by a well-manicured hand emerging from the car window as she triumphantly flipped us the bird. All of actions of the blond goddess were implausible and obviously unexplainable. What petty need did she seek to satisfy by making perfect strangers wait, unnecessarily, for a public parking space? To what end did this obviously privileged woman strive to empty a reservoir of petty frustrations, safely, against an undeserving group of strangers? My friend and I were shocked by the behavior of this obviously privileged and bored goddess. The whole situation was bizarre because not one person exchanged and yet the Blonde Goddess decided that she had to insult perfect strangers. The brief encounter left my friend and I speechless. In fact a word didn't pass between us for a good ten minutes after the incident because we were stunned at the woman's obvious low-class and anti-social behavior.

My friend and I entered the cool inner sanctum that is Nordstrom's a bit mystified and confused. To this day, neither my friend nor I can understand why the pampered Blonde Goddess decided that it was socially acceptable for her to make five cars wait for her to pull out of and share a public spot. What sense of power did the Blonde Goddess derive from acting like a petty child? It was clear to the people in each of the five cars that she had no intention of vacating the spot because she was unable to or maybe she had to return to Nordstrom's to quickly pick-up something that she had forgotten. Both excuses somehow didn't satisfy the "why" of this outlandish situation. It is clear that we didn't understand the motives of the Blonde Goddess any better than any one else and that is probably a very good thing. There is only thing that I am certain of: my friend isn't and will never be a goddess.

Unfortunately, this type of rude and provocative behavior from goddesses is more common than might be expected. The natural barriers that exist between men and women began to topple based on the bravado of the Feminist Movement that brought new words and their definitions to the social arena between men and women to try and describe the new outspoken, strong women who no longer needed men to fight their battles. Like many words that describe other human beings, the word most currently used to describe strong-willed, self-sufficient women, aggressive, is a word loaded word that is typically interpreted as negative if it is used to describe a woman or positive if it is used to describe a man. That being said let me be very clear. There is a group of women who engage in aggressive behavior that is typically directed against total strangers while they are in public places. These privileged princesses feel that they have the right to be rude, crude and nasty to others especially if they feel that they have been thwarted in some minor or major way. Let's examine another case of the unleashed social goddess in public.

It's a mild spring morning and my male next-door neighbor decides to take his dog to the local dog park for a romp. Many of the people who take their pets to the dog park tend to be civilized in the classical sense because they understand that animals like humans need outside activities to keep their lives interesting and fulfilled. Yet, on occasion, a few horror stories emerge about clearly uncivilized people who take their uncivilized dogs to a place where people and animals must be at their very best and vigilant or the people or their dogs will manage to cause havoc. Oftentimes, "dog park people" will encounter a goddess or two and the goddesses manage to spoil the experience for everyone at the park, including the dogs.

Our neighbor's dog is a Staffordshire terrier. Unlike most pit bulls, my neighbors' dog is not a large pit; his legs are long and graceful and his head and chest are not broad and muscular like typical pits. But he is a pit none-the-less. Unlike the endless negative propaganda that fills the airwaves about pit bulls, my neighbor's dog is extremely friendly and the only thing that might be judged as a negative about the dog's personality is that it believes that he is an eight year old boy. My neighbor feeds his dog's misperception about being a real boy by buying him remote control cars instead of doggie Frisbees. The other interesting fact about this very human like pit bull is that he resembles the pig in "Babe." He is an albino with freckles on his nose, tummy and eyelids. He is the cutest thing anyone in our neighborhood has seen and all of the neighborhood kid and their parents love him. Like his owner, the dog is patient and well-mannered even though he is spoiled beyond all reason.

My neighbor cooks the dog's food daily. His favorite is chicken thighs although I have seen him eat almost anything my neighbor's wife cooks and that includes spinach quiche. The couple has raised this dog since it was a puppy and it has never been put into a kennel and hr has never slept outside except when he was sprayed by a skunk and even then he slept on a pillow in their garage. The dog has more beds in their home than the residents. If the dog displayed any type of aggression, that is if you could call it aggression, only happens when he is separated from his family. His aggressive side is prone to crying and whining until his family returns. When his family leaves for a vacation or business, the pit is left with at least two people to visit him three times a day to feed, walk and to play with him to ensure his mental and physical well-being. Oh, and I did I mention that he swims daily as soon as the pool heats up?

It has been said that absence makes the heart grow fonder and in my neighbor's case with his best friend, the pit, this axiom holds true. When my neighbor returns, whether from a short or extended visit, my neighbor must deal with being licked all over by his dog; his ears, neck and as much of my neighbor's face as he'll allow for as long as he can stand it. The licking is a sing of gratitude in case you were wondering "why."

At the dog park, my neighbor's dog is typically always a gentle and amiable dog to humans and other dogs unless he is provoked or attacked by another dog. Unfortunately, he has been attacked on more than one occasion and some misguided dog park visitors are quick to judge my friend's dog as the instigator in any attack, even when it is perfectly clear that another dog was the aggressor. In other words, this media tainted animal is more humane than most of the people that I know.

Their day began as a typical day in suburbia. My neighbor "dressed" his dog, meaning he put the dog's harness on and then clipped on his leash, and headed for the park that co-joins the dog park with his New York Times tucked securely under his arm. A white cloud passed over the sun in an almost clear blue sky as if to foreshadow the coming doom or an approaching storm.

It didn't take long for my neighbor and his dog to arrive at the gate that separates the people's park from the dog park. My neighbor is retired although he doesn't look a day over forty. He is of medium height and most of the women in the neighborhood think that he is quite handsome. Many of the teens and preteens in the neighborhood think that he is a retired movie star. Anyway, this very handsome, and cultured man is greeted at the dog park fence by two wild and out of control young women under the age of thirty. Both are dressed in the traditional garb of the modern exercise fanatic who regularly visits their local gym. Both of the young women are either blond or have managed to create an abundance of blonde streaks in their auburn curls. These two young goddesses look as if they just stepped out of the pages of an exercise magazine for women. Except their cover-girl image is marred by the two braying at my neighbor, spittle flying from their perfect little mouths flying, at the top of their lungs!

Not only are these goddesses braying at him at the top of their lungs but they have also physically wedged themselves against the fence that leads to the entrance to the dog park. The action of these two goddesses clearly prohibited my neighbor and his dog from entering the dog park. An aside is necessary at this point: neither of the two women resides in the city where the dog park is located and yet my neighbor is and has been a tax paying resident for well over twenty years in this suburb outside of Los Angeles.

Not only are these two supposedly refined goddesses screaming at the top of their lungs but one of these 'docile' and obviously sweet goddesses had never even been to the dog park in our fair city before. But wait…stop the presses: not only had this fair damsel never met my neighbor or his dog before that day but she also didn't own a dog! Think about the size of the balls that this goddess thought that she had allowed her to confront and insult a perfect stranger who just so happens to be a grown and elegant man!

So, here is this visiting goddess at a public facility, without a dog, and yet she managed to ascertain that she was appointed dog-park cop and had the right to prohibit a regular visitor from entering the local public dog park. The goddess was unmoved by the fact that she was prohibiting a tax-paying resident from bringing his dog into the dog park because her friend had told her that she was disturbed by and didn't like pit bulls. It didn't matter that my neighbor and his dog had better manners than either of these two goddesses.

Media inspired, the two goddesses decided to launch an attack against my neighbor and his dog. It also didn't matter that the Dog Park Goddess was known to be a negligent owner who spent most of her time at the dog park time on her cell phone rather than paying attention to her unruly pups. Her dogs were people unfriendly and they were also dog unfriendly.. The only thing that mattered to the Visiting Goddess was that her friend, the Dog Park Goddess, was annoyed and unhappy with the presence of a pit bull in the park at the same time that she and her animals were in the park. The two goddesses, emboldened by their collective anger, were quite content with their decision to bar another person from the dog park, just because they didn't like the breed of dog. Never mind that either goddess knew nothing about my neighbor much less the character and attitude of his dog before they decided to bar them from the park.

Unlike the two jackasses; oh, I'm sorry, I meant to say goddesses at the dog park, my neighbor, being a man graced with incredible people skills and way too much savvy decided that the two goddesses weren't worth spoiling his morning paper. Neither of those two cretins could ever hope to acquire the moxie that my neighbor had in he tip of his little finger even if they had managed to live three lifetimes.

My neighbor, without a word to the two screaming goddesses, left the entrance gate to the dog park voluntarily. He crossed the street with his distinctive erect posture, dog in tow and left in his "dog" car to take his dog to the local mountain streams and canyons, instead.

Just how is it be possible for two women to bar a man and his dog from entering a park that his tax dollars paid for without experiencing just a little guilt? How is it possible for one unthinking goddess to accosti unknown male and his dog at the dog park, a decorated ex-Marine who fought in Vietnam without the slightest bit of shame? How can these two women brazenly deny him entrance to a park in the United States of America, a park and an ideal that he fought to preserve for them and the millions of others that he would never know. These two goddesses would never think about taking up a gun and placing their lives on the line in his or anyone else's defense? How could these two rude and contentious women have the temerity to insult a person who was so obviously much older, an honorable man, who had defended their right to be free Americans to travel where they pleased without constraint, deny him the same rights that they enjoyed?

These blonde-goddess darlings assumed that it was their right to bar my neighbor and his dog from the local public dog park because they didn't like the dog's breed. It's kind of like people deciding that they don't like black, Asian or Latin people simply because of their race. Dogs are just like people in that they shouldn't be judged on breed alone. Like people, dogs learn to be either vicious or loving. It would appear that the goddesses missed that day in school where this specific part of common sense should have been taught.

The Visiting Goddess decided that the observations and prejudices of her friend were enough to launch her into a physical attack against a complete male stranger. The Visiting Goddess trusted her friend's word without verifying whether or not her friend had a valid point of view; the Visiting Goddess just chose to act without thought. Who other than a misguided goddess would walk around and relate to other people in the world with an alarming sense of entitlement that just so happened to place her in harms way, simply on the "say-so" of a friend? All goddesses enjoy a clear sense of entitlement and power that allows them to practice manipulation against other women or men without guilt. Goddesses appear to operate without a moral compass and many drape the flag of feminism around their amoral behaviors with the hope of deflecting censure and exposure.

The two park goddesses surely relied on the fact that they appeared to be practicing feminists. They drove to place that they considered safe; a dog park in an upscale suburban neighborhood. In other words, the goddesses dropped into the neighborhood and decided that they had enough power to dictate their desires to other people without fear of reprisals or possible physical harm.

After the fact, some personal information about the Dog Park Goddess came to light after my neighbor's non-verbal confrontation. Dog park people are just like other people. People 'share' information about the behavior of certain dog's and their owners with other dog park regulars.

The Dog Park Goddess lived in an apartment with her two dogs in a nearby city. The Dog Park Goddess tried to bring her dogs to the park several days a week, during the morning, because her time to report for work was late morning. The only time that the Dog Park Goddess's dogs left the confines of her apartment was before she went to work. What a sad, confined and lonely life those dogs must lead. Those two dogs spend hours a day confined in a small space without stimulation or room to run, play or explore their environment. Add to that dreary scenario the fact that these two animals have very little contact with their human or other human beings. It's no wonder that those dogs are uncivilized; nothing has been done to effectively civilize them.

Over the years my neighbor has endured many confrontations at the dog park at the behest goddess dog owners. Most of these braying, spittle spewing goddesses are almost always distracted because they are on heir cell phones instead of paying attention to their dogs and their behavior with other dogs and the other humans at the dog park. To avoid further confrontation, my neighbor has adopted a new routine: he rarely if ever takes his dog to the local dog park. He has learned to avoid the local dog park not only for his dog's safety but for his safety and well-being as well.

It appears as if dog etiquette is another subject that should be taught to perspective dog owners before people are allowed to own and commune with other civilized owners and their dogs. The only thing that self-centered goddesses inspire in most civilized people is ire and frustration because goddesses really do believe that they are an invaluable facet of society and are therefore more privileged and entitled to judge, rant, rave or insult perfect strangers in very public places. But the saga of insulting goddesses doesn't end at the dog park.

There is an all too typical female habit that is at once infectious and demeaning. Whatever another woman thinks about other people or issues, certain women will take the word of a female friend and even the word of a TV personality as gospel without thinking or even asking for some form of proof. Many grown women have easy access to their former middle school hurts and slights and are psychologically and emotionally confined to responding immaturely to serious adult situations because their play book responses were formed when they were pre-teens. Therefore many goddesses spend a lot time inappropriately expressing themselves to other less-than secure women about issues and people they have no personal or credible knowledge, yet the goddesses will decide to take a negative stance against another person based on scant information from another woman. For far too many women, the word of a "trusted" friend is more than enough for them to be rude or nasty to other people. If Oprah on her celebrated TV show makes a statement about someone on her show, say an endorsement for a book, then it follows that Oprah's book needs to be read, right? Well, all endorsements are not solely Oprah's. Ms. Winfrey has a cadre of producers whose job requires them to come up with interesting and pertinent ideas for the show ideas. Many of these ideas for shows may or many not have anything to do with fact or reality. Since a lot of women accept what they "see" on television as gospel, many of those women live unexamined lives and what they see is never examined. Unfortunately, for the rest of us, places where people normally congregate like parks and grocery stores have become landmines for the common man or woman who foolishly ventures into the land of the goddesses.

It was another bright and sunny perfect day in southern California. It really is almost impossible for the days not to be perfect and sunny in southern California but then of course, southern California is also populated by an abundance of goddesses who ensure that someone's perfect day will end quite badly.

The neighborhood might be considered upscale in certain areas of the country because the median home price for a small (less than 1400 sq. ft.) two-bedroom, one-bath home is quite a bit more than $700,000.00. Homes that are larger than 2,000 sq. ft. are in the million dollar range, but this is southern California where real estate values are sky high and a lot of people drive mega SUV's. The streets during the day are filled with mothers driving those pricey SUV's or some pricey foreign sedan or station wagons. If you're a wise person you'll avoid driving by the local elementary or middle schools during the hours when children arrive or depart from school. The surrounding streets are full of mothers jockeying those oversized vehicles into small spaces as they drop-off or pick-up their pampered, privileged and often rude children.

Saturday in this Southern Californian suburb is like most suburban family communities across America. Saturday tends to be market and chore day. An aerial shot of the local grocery store parking lot on Saturday afternoons resembles a gleaming array of close fitting, shiny beetles. Visiting the local market late mornings or early afternoons on Saturday is not recommended to the faint of heart. Another one of my male neighbor's, a weekend soccer referee, needed to restock his referee bag with a few bottles of Gatorade to ensure that his body remained properly hydrated for his long afternoon of scheduled games. Poor, poor misguided man! Without a doubt, he should have avoided the grocery store and spent a few more coppers at the local 7-Eleven.

My neighbor's Saturday afternoon saga actually began before he arrived at the grocery store parking lot. The store is just a few blocks from our homes but he was in a bit of a hurry to get to the field to ref his games. He grabbed his sports bag full of his gear and determined that he was all out of Gatorade. He checked the pantry and the garage but his search was in vain. So, he jumped into his weekend car and drove to the local market, expecting to be able to get in and get out quickly.

My neighbor waited patiently at the red light at a nearby busy intersection, his fingers' drumming on the steering wheel to the beat of The Rolling Stones. He waited patiently for the light to change so that he could drive across the well-traveled boulevard. The light turned green and he tapped the accelerator and his weekend car sprang to life. Half-way through the intersection he slowed to anticipate the dips in the road and the entrance to the grocery store parking lot. While negotiating a right turn into the lot, he was suddenly cut-off by a woman turning left into the parking lot in front of him. To avoid hitting the SUV, my neighbor had to really slam on the brakes to ensure a hard stop. The driver in the SUV cast a furtive look in his direction as she sped in front of him. My neighbor couldn't help but to yell: "Hey! Be careful."

Dust and small rocks kicked-up in front of his car and windshield in the wake of the SUV into the parking lot in front of him. Jolted by the aggressive and dangerous maneuver made by the woman in the darting SUV, my neighbor decided it was necessary for him to give a friendly warning after he parked his car. He thought misguidedly, "Maybe that person didn't see me."

So, this kind and gentle man parked his beat-up, old weekend car and ambled over to the driver of the SUV. He noticed as he approached the SUV that the driver was a woman and that she was yelling at someone, possibly in the car with her. She had rolled down her window and she was yelling, he assumed, at someone either in the back of the SUV or at someone behind him. He was now confident that the SUV driver hadn't seen him when she made that dangerous turn into the parking lot and managed to get the last prime parking space.

Before my neighbor could even greet the "lady" driver, let's call her La Crazy Driving Goddess, she boiled out of her SUV in a rage. Being a healthy and athletic male in his mid-forties, my neighbor couldn't help but to notice that the lady was intentionally assaulting him verbally. My neighbor was a bit shocked by the woman's anger. Being a red-blooded male, the woman's voice faded into the background as he admired her physical attributes. She was endowed with perfect features and a very voluptuous body. The beauty before him stood about 5'7" tall. Her face was flawless complimented by high cheek bones and a full mouth. Her body was well-toned and tanned. Her breasts were not large, but ample. Although her eyes were shooting darts of fire at him as he approached her he just couldn't manage to take his eyes off her shapely, almost perfect legs. The poor man completely missed the woman's vexed expression and he stopped hearing the words the fell freely from her mouth as if she were his wife.

Poor misguided male. He was actually attracted to this goddess in spite of her spoiled brat act. Men! La Crazy Driving Goddess strolled up to my neighbor squared her shoulders, placed her hands on her slender hips and lashed-out and shouted at him. Her intent was all too obvious; she was hoping to draw attention and a crowd to her and this made-up situation . "How dare you! Do you know that you almost killed me? You're an idiot!" My neighbor was shocked and taken aback by the onslaught of the now venom that spewed at him from the woman. Her tone and manner snapped him back into reality and out of semi-infatuation. My neighbor decided that it was far better for him to back away from this goddess regardless of how good she looked. Besides, his rational side was screaming "she almost killed me!" My neighbor began his exit and almost backed into the store. He decided the best thing for him to do was to just back away and into the store.

He backed away from her and into the safety and anonymity of the crowded store. La Crazy Driving Goddess should have received an Oscar for her performance that day because it was definitely over the top. It's amazing how this well-groomed, attractive "lady" could have ever thought that it was okay to walk-up to a perfect stranger and insult him in a public setting. As he attempted to ease into the store the goddess continued her attack. A crowd had formed as she continued to fling verbal insults at him from her perfectly glossed lips. In goddess like acumen, she quickly assessed that my neighbor was a "nice" guy and feeling safe she decided to make her insults more personal: "You're just a dickless asshole!" The amazing thing was that the "lady" showed no shame during this very public tirade and all because she was miffed because my neighbor had the audacity to caution her about her aggressive and reckless driving habits. But my neighbors embarrassing encounter in front of the store in the parking lot didn't end there.

Inside the store, La Crazy Driving Goddess continued to launch her assault against him. She made a beeline for the manager's desk that was located at the front of the store. The man standing behind the desk was in his late fifties, balding, nondescript. His tie was slightly unloosened and his attention was on the slow moving check-out stands in front of him. Before the man was able to focus on her, La Crazy Driving Goddess began her fast-paced verbal demand for help from the startled manager.

To the surprised and unsuspecting manager the goddess was at once beautiful and helpless as she related her tale to him about being harassed by a man in the parking lot. The Crazy Driving Goddess demanded that the manager help her to find the man who had insulted her and to throw him out of the store so that she could feel safe while shopping. Overwhelmed by her vehemence, the manager had no choice but to accompany the woman in her search. As the two approached the fruit and vegetable aisle the Crazy Goddess saw my neighbor's back as he rounded the opposite side of the long corridor. Spying my neighbor for that fleeting moment, La Crazy Driving Goddess managed to stop, place her hand on the manager's should while she pointed at my neighbor's retreating back as her chin trembled ever so slightly. That slight tremble reached across the void between La Crazy Driving Goddess and the manager and lodged itself in the prince charming alter ego of the grocery store manager. This alter ego required the store manager to always protect a damsel in distress.

The problem with the manager's faulty logic was that this was no lady and she surely didn't need male protection. La Crazy Driving Goddess cinched the rouse by managing to dredge up some tears that pushed the manager's protective gene into overdrive. His pace quickened as he hurried off to apprehend the ingrate who had insulted the obviously defenseless and beautiful damsel. My neighbor had managed to disappear down an aisle way at the back of store as the manager followed him in hot pursuit.

The manager was obviously a man with a mission as he strode determinedly towards my neighbor. The manager assumed the role as alpha male and began by tapping the accused male on the shoulder and demanding that he explain his actions towards the woman in the parking lot. My neighbor stopped his forward progress in mid-stride and turned towards the store manager. As La Crazy Driving Goddess arrived on the scene, the manager recognized my neighbor as being one of his long-time, loyal customers. The manager's anger dissipated instantly. The manager suddenly became uncertain about who exactly had offended La Crazy Driving Goddess in the parking lot. He couldn't help but to think: "It couldn't be Mr. Smith." The only course of action that the manager could comfortably pursue was to greet his customer cordially: "Hey Tom, how's it going?" My neighbor responded guardedly because La Crazy Driving Goddess had stopped right beside the manager and looked up at the man beseechingly.

The manager turned towards La Crazy Driving Goddess and asked incredulously: "You can't mean this man?" La Crazy Driving Goddess paused dramatically and stood so physically close to the manager that he felt and smelled the warmth of her body. The smell of her, so near to him, almost made the man swoon. Her smell was enhanced by a mix of an expensive, exotic perfume and her natural pheromones. La Crazy Driving Goddess tried to position her body even closer to the manager's, as if that was humanly possible, and looked up at him with a slight chin tremble and whispered: "Yes," with a truly shaken voice, "that's him!" Trapped by the goddess on one side and by a loyal customer on the other, the manager became noticeably uncomfortable. A slight sheen of sweat broke-out on the manager's upper lip and it became clear that he was torn between the beautiful damsel in distress and his loyal customer. The man could barely summon the strength to question his loyal customer about the accusations lodged against him by La Crazy Driving Goddess. The manager nervously cleared his throat and croaked out: "Ah, hey Tom, just how... how are you this afternoon?" My neighbor nodded at the manager and watched as the goddess waited for the manager to lower the boom. The manager instantly became aware of the riding tension in the air added to my neighbor's unmistakable male stance that signaled to him that my neighbor was not in a friendly mood.

The manager shrank back from the tone of my neighbor's voice which was very dry. The manager was a man who disliked confrontation but the situation before him was dicey at best because he didn't relish having to choose between the beautiful goddess and one of his best customer. My neighbor's overall tenor and tone made the manager extremely uncomfortable. The manager continued nervously: "Ah…I'm sorry, but this lady" the volume of his voice trailed and softened to the point that it almost disappeared into the surrounding noise of a busy Saturday afternoon. To repeat, my neighbor is a classy and patient man therefore he decided to rescue the poor manager who was obviously dangling by a string in mid-air over a very dangerous precipice. My neighbor kept an eye on La Crazy Driving Goddess and told the manager about the preceding sad saga: "Listen Bob, let's cut to the chase. I think you better call the police to settle this situation."

Just as La Crazy Driving Goddess heard the word "police," she became alarmed and began to make motions as if she were trying to escape: "Ah, I don't think we need to call the police!" The manager noticed that the woman had begun to physically move away from him. To increase the distance between them, the manager took a few steps away from her and what he considered to be the line of fire from my neighbor. La Crazy Driving Goddess perceived that the manager's testosterone levels had peaked and were in decline so she rushed in an attempt to repair the splintering situation; she continued a bit too quickly with: "I'm sure that it was just a misunderstanding." My neighbor completely ignored her half-hearted apology and the fact that she had even spoken: "Bob. Take this." My neighbor handed his cell phone to the manager. "Call the PD now, please. You know they'll be here in less than five minutes." The manager took my neighbor's cell phone with shaky hands and began to key in the digits to the local police. As he entered the numbers La Crazy Driving Goddess backed away quickly and quietly from the two men and disappeared down the aisle and out through the front doors and into obscurity.

And that's the problem with all those goddesses who bustle about town, each caught up in their own private world that is usually devoid of real people that they consider worthwhile. Goddesses, by nature, are completely unaware that other people have needs and desires unless of course those other people can provide them with some sort of valuable service. Of course many goddesses are simply happy just have a close coterie of people who simply live to dance to their tunes. These goddesses have no sense of common courtesy or decorum that should flow easily between people. Goddesses believe that respectful behavior and/or concerns for other people are acts that apply solely to the behaviors of other people towards them. Goddesses generally judge the people in their lives based on whether they might fulfill some current or future use.

The privileged Goddess/Diva mentality has produced a new class of modern goddesses who are far from being the archetypical definition of what being a gentlewoman should be all about. Although many goddesses feign helplessness and fragileness, goddesses rarely if ever need protection from anyone in most situations because most are master manipulators. In fact, the ugly truth is that most of the rest of us are woefully ill-equipped to deal with an expertly conceived plan set into motion by a goddess. Although most of us smile and deny that we have ever been burned and hurt by individual encounters with a goddess, most of us still carry the emotional scars left on our souls by goddesses. Most women have suffered at least one unpleasant experience at the hands of a goddess and most of us also know that we are all destined to continue to endure those smiling, poisoned tongued, self-indulgent women until they learn that the rest of us will no longer tolerate or accept their negative behaviors. .

Now let's jump forward a few light years. A near and very dear friend had just celebrated ten years of marriage to a very nice guy. The two of them had agreed to put off starting a family until after both had finished college; therefore their first child was born a few months after they celebrated their seventh year of marriage. Three years after the birth of the first child, the happy couple waited expectantly for the birth of their second child. As their fate would have it, their second child was born a mere three years and five days after the birth of their first child. Like most young couples with kids they were strapped for cash and had not yet purchased a home. As a young mother and housewife my friend had managed to avoid contact with goddesses. But her world was about to shift dramatically with the arrival of new tenants that had moved into their apartment complex. My friend is the "Welcome Wagon's" poster child and couldn't resist reaching out to the newly arrived young couple.

The guy part was a medium-sized, dark skinned, athletic African American with a brilliant and easy smile. She was almost petite except for her ample hips. She also had flashing blue eyes and short, auburn curls. Although the surrounding neighborhood was well integrated, a mixed marriage was still a social anomaly. The young woman's pensive face and stiff posture tugged at my friend's heartstrings as the mothering hormones filled her being. Let's just say that the rush of hormones must have clouded my friend's judgment about people or maybe she was really tired of solely communicating most days with a three year old whenever she wasn't busy vomiting into a nearby trash can. Ah, pregnancy and its many wonders! Or maybe the poor dear was just plain lonely.

Whatever the reason, my friend's reason was blinded by, let's call her the Nurse Goddess. The Nurse Goddess wasn't a beauty; in fact she was more like the girl next door type. The one thing that stood out about the Nurse Goddess was that she was, in a word, very cute. My friend on the other hand felt she looked like a beached whale although she was really a very beautiful pregnant woman. My friend is petite, very well built and she manages, damn her, to only gain nineteen pounds with each of her three cherubs. From the rear, my friend never resembled what other pregnant women look like, ungainly and broad assed. At eight months pregnant, my friend still had lots of guys trying to pick her up, that is, when she wasn't visibly and audibly up-choking. My friend and the Nurse Goddess also became friends because my friend had to walk by the goddess's apartment to climb the stairs to her second story unit.

A month after the arrival of Nurse Goddess and her man, my friend delivered her second child. The Nurse Goddess and her young man married and once they made their union known to her stunned and angry family, the two basically ceased contact with her family. My friend, her husband and her small brood found a home to purchase in a nearby suburb after the birth of their son. The couples parted but managed to maintain a distant relationship that was based on chess games between the guys and "girl talk" between the two women.

It wasn't long before I began to notice that my friend was always a bit blue after a visit with the Nurse Goddess and her husband. My friend revealed that the Nurse Goddess had acquired a new habit since she and her family had moved; i.e., every time my friend and her husband visited the Nurse Goddess or vice versa, the Nurse Goddess always managed to deliver several well-placed verbal digs at my friend. Each barb was always followed by the Nurse Goddess giggling or delivering a quip that was meant to cover-up the barb that always found its mark in my friend's heart.

At first, my friend thought that the Nurse Goddess was just being passive/aggressive. My friend reasoned that the Nurse Goddess was obviously delivering misdirected criticism and pain to my friend. My friend learned to laugh nervously while being verbally assaulted by the Nurse Goddess. As nice as my friend is as a person, she can also be a bit slow on the uptake. Stop the presses, maybe that why she and I are friends. My friend is the last person in the world to assume that someone is out to "get" her. It literally took several years for my friend to fully comprehend that the Nurse Goddess was actually covertly attacking her. My friend just couldn't come to terms with the fact that the Nurse Goddess was simply being mean and that she enjoyed playing her one-sided, pointed game to undermine my friend's emotional well-being. What my friend couldn't accept was that the Nurse Goddess had more fun destroying her self-confidence than in simply ending the relationship.

And this is one of the classic ways of identifying a true goddess: it's always better to maintain a relationship with someone based on abuse or use rather than developing real relationships with real people. The Nurse Goddess was also blessed with a dry wit and a disarming smile. Just picture Ann Coulter after launching what she considers to be the coup de grace against a hated liberal adversary and you'll have an excellent idea of what the Nurse Goddess's smile looked like whenever after she emotionally stabbed my friend. As a registered nurse it would have been perfectly normal for her to cultivate her friendships exclusively with other nurses but the Nurse Goddess preferred spending time with other women as well. It appeared to me as if the Nurse Goddess felt superior to my friend and that she oddly felt inferior to other nurses, especially those who had managed to marry doctors.

The relationship between my friend and the Nurse Goddess hadn't been a great one for years. In fact the relationship was almost non-existent. But the game of cat and mouse began to wane as my friend regained her senses and realized that the Nurse Goddess was anything but a friend. As my friend began to decline invitations from the Nurse Goddess, the Nurse Goddess switched from being benignly quiet to venomous, insulting tirades against my friend.

The saddest thing was that it took almost fifteen years for the relationship to fizzle. Their so-called relationship had never even been a so-so friendship. For years, my friend was plagued with not knowing exactly what made the Nurse Goddess dislike her. For my friend it was like she was back in high school again. My friend felt that she was once again ridiculed and abandoned by the popular group. She was shamed, even as an adult woman, not to be considered "good enough" to be befriended by the Nurse Goddess. I tried to help my friend to understand what it was about her personality that made her seek out hurtful, emotional relationships with people who clearly didn't care about her. It was clear that my friend was conflicted by and hurt by her misperceptions that she wasn't good enough to establish a meaningful relationship with the Nurse Goddess.

After many, many years had passed, my friend finally acknowledged that she wasn't at fault in this broken relationship. My friend was finally able to see that the fault, if there was one, was inside of the Nurse Goddess. Once my friend was able to accept the truth of the situation she was finally able to finally move away from that toxic relationship and heal.

And whatever happened to the Nurse Goddess? Well, as far as I know she is still out there wreaking havoc on other women's lives just for a laugh. Like most women, my friend spent a lot of time trying to figure out what was wrong with her instead of realizing that the other person in the relationship has a responsibility to try and maintain a healthy, satisfying relationship. My friend has something specific in common with a lot of women: for women it's just easier for them to accept that relationships fail because they are at fault in some minor or major way. Whether a woman is abused emotionally or physically, many women accept the yoke of responsibility if a relationship flounders.

Goddesses, on the other hand, are clearly never responsible for relationship failures. It never occurred to my friend that the Nurse Goddess had never intended, from the very beginning, to be her friend. Unfortunately, my friend was a mother with children of her own yet her adult experience in life didn't stop or shield her from experiencing years of self-doubt and uncertainty after this relationship ended. She was literally confounded by the behavior a person who intentionally misused her and eventually discarded her like she was no better than a used tissue.

Like many women in failed relationships with other women, my friend assumed that the Nurse Goddess was perfect while the Nurse Goddess was clearly imperfect as a prospect for friendship. And that is the real power that the goddesses hold over the rest of us: accepted group perfection over only perceived imperfection. All Goddesses have an aura of confidence that translates to the rest of the world as goodness and a sense of caring about others, when in fact the mark of a mean goddess can be assessed by only observing how much time these women spend undermining other women, their family members and their co-workers.

There is a vein of bright sunshine that illuminates and warms my friend's heart at the end of this tale: my friend hasn't spoken to or had contact with the Nurse Goddess in almost a decade. The Nurse Goddess and her chocolate candy bar man faded into the sands of time. The pain that my friend experienced from the failure of this relationship has also faded, although my friend has a sense of sadness in her heart for what might have been rather than what never could have been.

The Enigma of That Winning Smile
Chapter 9

Everyone agrees that there's nothing more endearing and uplifting in life than seeing a beautiful smile. There's something about the human face that emits an inner glow when a person smiles. Even the most hardhearted of us appear to melt and relax just a bit when confronted by a perfect smile especially if that smile is flashed by a child. And if that smile is genuine it seems as if spring blooms and fills the air with the sweet smell of flowers with a sun kissed warmth that brightens the darkest corners of our souls while the obvious poetry and beauty of the smile work its silent magic.

Genuine smiles can be found everywhere all around us everyday. Smiles are not very difficult to find; just take the time to look around. Maybe if you're lucky you will be able to spy an infectious, spontaneous source of smiles on the faces of young children. The smiles on the faces of the young are almost always charming and heartwarming despite the fact that many of these cherub's are clearly missing more than a few pearly whites. Yet the beauty and innocence of these unfettered and unpretentious smiles shine clearly and the smiles of the very young rarely fail to warm even the coldest of hearts. Other smiles that tend to warm the heart can be found on the faces of the very old. The smiles of the aged are sometimes worn and haggard but once an old persons eyes begin to twinkle, their paper-thin skin folds into age-worn wrinkles as their lips spread apart to release a burst of energy that almost whisks away the years of pain as the past disintegrates into an often toothless grin.

So, the smile alone can be a force of nature even when self-conscious teens display their glistening braces or their broad and toothy uneven grins to friends or would- be admirers; the act of smiling seems to erase the scowls that covers their faces. Brides and grooms of every age cast nervous smiles at one another during the most important ceremony of their lives. When babies enter the world most people can't contain their joy or their wonder at the special new arrival. And then of course there are the smiles cast by the goddess class. Ah, and what a marvel such a thing has become.

Traditionally, women use and have used their smiles to disarm tense situations. Women use their smiles as a signal to men in public places to let them know that they are interested in him. The smile of a woman is known to be a potent aphrodisiac. Mothers from all over the globe have used their smiles to sooth and dry the tears of their little ones who may have fallen and incurred a "boo-boo." Mothers also use their smiles to encourage a fearful child not to be afraid or to simply greet an old family member or friend.

Although the smile has been used to inspire and warm cold hearts but smiles are also used influence, engender trust and to affect manipulation of the worst type. To think that someone could consciously misuse such a beautiful human characteristic is difficult. But Goddesses are known for their perfect smiles and goddesses have managed to have managed to corrupt the smile for cruel and dastardly deeds.

Now the smile of a goddess is just as disarming as any other genuine smile that you might encounter in your daily life. The smile of a goddess is totally disarming while also being wholly disingenuous. The smiles employed by the goddesses of the world causes more harm and pain than any other destructive habit used by others to further their own agendas whether for economic gain, simple personal aggrandizement or to draw more attention to oneself at the expense of someone else.

Please let there be no doubts about the smiles used by goddesses to either extract favors from other people or to inflict pain on others; the smile of the goddess, when used properly, is almost always accompanied by a hefty emotional price tag that has to be paid for by the rest us. Let's start by identifying some well-known goddesses whose flashy smiles dazzle and flash across the flickering silver screens and fill us all with peace, trust and tranquility. Not!

So, let's start with a not-so-sweet, sharp-tongued female who decided that she's the meanest and nastiest female political commentator on national television and in national print. It appears that this goddess is extremely comfortable with her professional life as the Queen of Mean in that she is allowed to be indescribably provocative and mean to other people who don't embrace her particular brand of politics. This goddess gets-off on insulting and maligning the characters of other people in her quest to remain the darling of an exclusive political cabal, the neo-conservatives. This woman only enjoys eviscerating other people and she has been allowed to flourish in the media in spite of her vile statements while flashing her perfect goddess-like smile as she makes fun of her chosen opponents' painful life circumstances or by making disgraceful comments about the tragic death of someone's beloved child. Wicked Goddess has gleefully hoped that one or more adversaries of her and her neo-conservative ideology might, wink and smile real sweetly, lose their lives in a terrorist attack. Her most brutal attacks are always accompanied by that winning, frost-biting smile. This self-righteous and emotionless goddess earns her money on the tit of the provocatively absurd and yet she flourishes. The Goddess Ann Coulter uses that golden goddess smile every time she lodges an attack against a liberal or any well-meaning individual inclined to use thought and logic in a search for truth, concepts that clearly escaped Coulter's incisive inability to fully address any issues without her actively delving into character assassination. The Goddess Ann Coulter is renowned for her cutting invectives and insensitive verbal attacks against anyone she perceives as a likely target for her venom and vituperative condescension. The Goddess Coulter inclines her perfectly coiffed head of long blonde hair just a tad before she delivers that smile that is always filled with infamy. If you look closely, something I don't recommend for the faint of heart, you'll discover that Coulter's smile is actually a grimace rather than a real smile.

Yet, the Goddess Coulter uses the disarming weapon of the female smile much like hundreds of thousands of little girls all across the globe who have learned to use their smiles to deal with emotional rejection or to disarm an enemy, typically an enraged male, before an attack. Like all of the other goddesses that the world has spawned, the Goddess Coulter uses her smile in much the same way that other women have used their smiles for eons. A smile is the female's most prized possession and weapon, or more appropriately, the female's ultimate heart softener.

It's important to remember that almost all little girls are taught to smile real pretty every time someone asks her to take her picture or when the little miss has to greet relatives and/or total strangers. Little girls have always been taught to smile even though they have no reason to smile. If little girls have their feelings hurt by a little friend or if they are disappointed rather than throw a fit, little girls are encouraged by their moms or grandma's to smile because all little girls are raised and taught to be "well-mannered and well-behaved" no matter how much their little hearts are breaking. Little girls learn to smile during times of stress and even during times of fear because they have learned how to respond to these negative situations from their mothers or grandmothers, adult strong women in their lives who have great influence over their lives and have in turn, influenced their behaviors and their lives. Little girls have learned from the other women in their lives, who are also paragons of strength, to smile even when their little bodies hurt. The sad thing is that most little girls trundle off to school with their collective emotions too big for their little bodies to contain and sometimes these little girls have experienced physical or emotional abuse that result in fears that leave them with deep, crusted-over emotional scars that are exemplified by tight, terror-ridden grimaces that are supposed to resemble smiles. Some little girls are so burdened with pain that is buried deeply inside of their little souls that their little faces almost crack when they attempt to smile because of all of the pain hidden deep within. The smiles on these little girls' faces simply lie on the surfaces of their faces just as if they were papier mache dolls. Unfortunately, some of these fake smiles are flashed just to calm their mothers' nerves or merely to keep other people at bay.

Once upon a time not so very long ago a young lady entered the life of a very dear friend. My friend was the proud mother of three very lively, healthy and completely different children. Her brood was comprised of two girls and a boy. Her middle child is the boy. Like most women who have healthy and adventurous sons, my friend's life was filled with an ample amount of surprise mixed-in with ample amounts of fear mostly because of her beloved son. Unlike many of his friends, let's just call him the Prince, the Prince managed to continue to live under his parent's roof until he was almost twenty-five years old. And then one light-filled and sunny day he met the woman of his dreams. Or so he thought.

Let's talk briefly about the attributes of the young Prince. First of all, my friend's son is a heartthrob. He has a broad, perfect and easy grin and he is so completely comfortable with women of all ages that it is almost as if he were an old soul who returned just to tickle, tease and pleasure all women. Throughout his teen years, my friend's home was always filled with expectant and infatuated young women and it seemed to me whenever I visited the home that the house phone never stopped ringing. So, it was surprising for all of us to learn that this paragon of masculinity had finally fallen for an unknown temptress.

At a pre-planned family dinner, my family and I along with my good friend met the prospective temptress, to forever be known as the Dream Goddess. My friend and I have been friends for well over twenty-years. Our friendship is a testament to one of those odd occurrences that happen, only occasionally, between two strong and vital women. So, because of our established mutual friendship over the years our two separate households have come together and we have been "family" to each other for decades. Therefore it was only natural for the Dream Goddess to be thoroughly inspected by both families.

The first meeting with the Dream Goddess was simultaneously interesting and boring because the Dream Goddess managed to appear, at least on the surface, to be the perfect woman for my friend's son. Ms. Dream Goddess managed to execute every social move correctly. When I closed my eyes it was like I was transported to the set of "The Philadelphia Story" and the Dream Goddess was Katherine Hepburn before she got drunk. Although the Dream Goddess wasn't what any of us considered a raving beauty, she was outgoing and warm with a bubbling personality. The truth is that she bordered on being manic but she was also overly polite. She possessed a dazzling, enormous smile which she managed to somehow flash at everyone constantly. My friend was the epitome of the ever watchful mother, looking for the hidden flaws in this paragon of femininity. Besides, the Dream Goddess was threatening to take away the Prince. This was the very first time in our long-standing relationship that I ever saw my usually warm and embracing friend standoffish while her two daughters exhibited the same signs of being distant and cold to their brother's new heart throb.

Just a bit more personal information about my dear friend's family: My friend, the lucky dog, managed to marry a drop-dead gorgeous man. Hence their progeny are all stunningly attractive and high-spirited children. The girls are exotically beautiful and both girls are blessed with an odd combination of beauty, strength and brains in today's world of media driven standards of beauty. Both are very hard-working in ways that suggests that neither girl is aware of her obvious physical attributes. Both of these young women are down to earth, blessed with a wicked sense of humor and it is obvious where and how their foundations were laid many years before.

The first meeting between the Prince and the Dream Goddess must have been magical. Apparently the initial meeting initiated a haze of sexual desire that required the two to be physically locked together in lust for the first several months of their relationship. And that's how long it took before the Prince was able to free himself from the sexual delights of the Dream Goddess long enough to arrange a meeting between her, his parents, and the rest of the 'family.'

So, the front door swung open on one quiet evening and the young Prince whisked the Dream Goddess into my friend's home. The Dream Goddess complimented my friend on the décor of her home and simply oozed feminine respect for the table settings to the preparations of and for the soon-to-be consumed meal. All the while the Dream Goddess managed to be extremely friendly and engaging to my friend and to her daughters. Oddly, the Dream Goddess was emotionally detached from the Prince. No matter, she must have been fully focused on bonding with the women of the family for a reason.

The Dream Goddess was of medium height with long, wiry auburn hair and olive complexion. Her skin is dark, a reflection of her not-so-distant gene pool with clear origins from Italy and Portugal. Her teeth are perfect and white. She is blessed with a slight feminine body and she appeared to hang onto every word spoken by my friend, her daughters or the occasional word added to the conversation by my friend's husband. Again, the Dream Goddess's manners were impeccable.

The young lady's past appears to be a bit checkered because at the moment she enjoys a distant relationship with her immediate family.

The Dream Goddess told my friend about her mom, dad, older sister and younger brother and that she had left home under a cloud. Her family lineage has been pivotal in her city's economic growth for well over a century. Before the Dream Goddess left home under a cloud, she fell in love with a young man that her family disliked and thoroughly mistrusted.

The Dream Goddess had escaped her family's censure a few years earlier and found out, much to her surprise, that her family's perception about that young man were correct. Once she left the protective arms of her family, the Dream Goddess said that she was routinely abused physically and mentally by the young man she thought was her prince charming. Like many abuse victims she harbored loads of shame and pain and the Dream Goddess explained that she didn't feel that she had the right to return to her parents' home without performing some form of penance. Guilt and maybe shame motivated the Dream Goddess not to accept any economic assistance from her family therefore she managed to attend college and live here without touching her numerous trust funds after the dissolution of her short-lived, violent affair.

After the break-up, the Dream Goddess immersed herself in college classes and full-time work. The Dream Goddess is apparently talented and exhibited an artistic sense of style that enabled her to create theme parties for adults and children. She also performed a fair job of being a wedding planner. The Dream Goddess, socially connected, always managed to arrange all of her affairs to be held at exclusive resorts and/or hotels.

It appeared as if all of the information that we ever wanted to know about the Dream Goddess, as well as all of the information that we never wanted to know was revealed to us that night. Much of the entire evening that extended long into the wee hours of the morning were filled with the Dream Goddess's droning voice as she brimmed over with discrete details about her private life. Obviously, her enthusiasm and willingness to over-indulge in self- revelation wasn't a crime in itself, but something was truly amiss because her intensity and enthusiasm about revealing simply everything on this first meeting was odd.

To further complicate the developing relationship between the two, the Prince and the Dream Goddess had met under unusual circumstances. The Prince's car was on the blink therefore he was relegated to hitching rides with friends until his car was fixed. On one particular afternoon the prince was trying to reach a male friend by cell phone to plead for a ride. The Prince dialed his friend's number and the call was answered by a young lady instead of his friend. The Prince inquired: "Say, ah... sorry, but is this Joe Blow's cell?" The Dream Goddess's reply was short and simple: "No!" Logically, the Prince assumed that he has misdialed and therefore redialed the number a second time. The Dream Goddess answered the number again. The two repeated the previous steps. On the third and final call, the Prince and the Dream Goddess were both stunned and a bit creeped-out that he had dialed the correct number three consecutive times and yet the connected call resulted in reaching the wrong number and person. Neither the Prince nor the Dream Goddess could understand how something so strange could have happened or how it happened three times in a row. What would be the odds if someone placed three consecutive calls to a specific number and that the Dream Goddess would answer all three miss-routed calls? Those odds have to be astronomical. The Dream Goddess believed, apparently the young lady is a true romantic at heart, that the coincidence was fate and decided that the two should meet, post haste. The Prince, a bit of a romantic himself, agreed that the two should meet in a well-lit public place just to ensure that there were cosmic forces at work in their lives.

Assuming that the Dream Goddess was a normal young woman, it seemed logical to think that she was keenly interested in finding a decent young man to fill her empty life. On the surface it appeared that either fate and/or serendipity were at work and that the young Prince had in fact met the woman of his dreams. Or so he thought, because in the end, the Dream Goddess managed to fulfill and destroy every dream that the Prince had ever dreamed.

Fast forward two and half years: my friend's eldest daughter had just announced her impending wedding. Of course her only brother's Dream Goddess had to be a part of the ceremony. The wedding, paid for entirely by my friend's daughter was elegant, beautiful and perfect. Let's call my friend's daughter the real Fairy Princess. The Fairy Princess chose to have her wedding and reception aboard a yacht. Trolling around the harbor was more than beautiful as the sun set and kissed the newly wedded couple with hues of gold, vermillion and electric blues. The food was excellent and the bride managed to have a blues singer and a small quartet in the downstairs lounge to entertain and a DJ on the upper deck boat to entertain the younger crowd. The Prince, although very inebriated, managed to collect the telephone numbers of all available young women at the reception and all of his shenanigans took place right under the watchful eye of the Dream Goddess. Needless to say the evening ended on an extremely tense note for the Prince and the Dream Goddess. A few short weeks later the Dream Goddess announced that she was pregnant.

The shock of her announcement reverberated throughout my friend's household. It was obvious to everyone in the household that the Prince was clearly unprepared for marriage and fatherhood. His actions at his sister's wedding also made it clear to the family that he was looking for a way to escape his relationship with the Dream Goddess. Instead, the Prince found himself proposing marriage to a woman that he cared for but wasn't really ready to make a life commitment to, at least at the moment. The situation intensified once the Dream Goddess made her parents' aware that they would soon be grandparents. The Dream Goddess came from a family of practicing Catholics therefore a marriage sanctioned by and performed in the Catholic liturgy between the Prince and the Dream Goddess was mandatory. The Prince's family were members of an even larger group; the ex-Catholics.

My friend was visibly upset about her son's upcoming nuptials. In fact she was absolutely certain that the Prince shouldn't marry the Dream Goddess because the Dream Goddess came from a very wealthy family and the class difference between the two families, she was certain, would eventually cause problems between the Prince and the Dream Goddess. To make matters even worse, the Prince and the Dream Goddess had been told by the Fairy Princess, that they were making a major mistake. The Fairy Princess knew that her baby brother wasn't ready for a lifelong commitment and that a baby wouldn't be enough to turn him into a mature husband and father.. But the Dream Goddess was intent on pursuing her dream of becoming a wife and mother and essentially told the Fairy Princess "Pshaw!" and continued on with her plans for an elaborate and expensive wedding.

Since the Dream Goddess was a few months along, the wedding had to take place quickly because the Dream Goddess had already managed to acquire that "mother-to-be" bulge because the Dream Princess also had an abiding love for food.

The big wedding day arrived and it was less than ideal. The sun was shining ever so brightly and it was ever so hot, actually it was boiling and it seemed as if the whole world would catch fire and burn. Everyone was hot and sweating and having to be dressed in formal attire for a formal affair was almost too much to bear. The heat didn't seem to affect the Dream Princess in the least as she flung orders at her mother and attendants to fulfill her very wish. The Dream Princess was simply giddy in her role of being "Bridezilla.".

To say that the wedding was expensive and oppressive would be an understatement. To say that the wedding was expensive might be the only positive thing that anyone could ever say or even remember about the whole affair. To begin with, the Dream Goddess decided that she simply needed twelve bridesmaids to be accompanied by twelve escorts. Every pew in the church was filled to capacity. The church glowed with the hot intensity because of an abundance of lit candles and every electric light burned brightly and increased the already high temperature another fifteen to twenty degrees. It was so hot the flowers in the church began to wilt.

The church hosted a near-capacity crowd the size of which is only matched when the believers feel the need for redemption on Christmas Eve and/or Easter Sunday. There were roughly four-hundred and fifty people in attendance. Less than twenty of the assembled guests had been invited by the groom and his family.

It was only to be expected that the bride and her wedding party would arrive late to the church for the ceremony despite the fact that her entourage arrived in two, air conditioned limousines. The Prince and his escorts found themselves abandoned in a sweltering, un-airconditioned room at the back of the church rectory while they waited for the arrival of the Dream Goddess and her twelve maidens. The bride and her maidens stepped from the limo's frosty cool while the groom and his escorts hastily wiped their dripping brows with handkerchiefs already soaked with sweat. The bride-to-be snapped at and managed to whip the overheated group of guys into order and the procession into the church proceeded without a hitch.

The wedding party proceeded down the aisle and finally assembled themselves on opposite sides of the altar; bridesmaids to the left and escorts to the right of the altar. The Dream Goddess beamed broadly while the groom's older sister, the Fairy Princess, sobbed audibly throughout the entire ceremony. The ceremony wasn't without a sense of high drama as the fully intoxicated priest couldn't control his need to kiss every woman that was within his reach. At some point during the eulogy, the priest's oversized Great Dane wandered down the church aisle and slobbered on a dozen guests. The painful experience of the wedding ceremony ended after a little more than an hour. But wait…. that wasn't the end of this saga.

The culmination of the wedding ceremony ended in endless staged photographs of the Dream Goddess, the Prince and their respective families. All of the guests were grateful to be out of the heat of the church whose thick stucco walls did not coolly affect and retard the heat of the day. It took all of the guests (think 450 hot people) just a few seconds to vacate the church in their quest to flee outdoors to what was assumed to be cooler air. But a blast of hot air greeted the sweat drenched revelers as they exited the church. That continuous blast of hot wind assured the guests that the evening festivities would be hot, sticky and uncomfortable. The evening reception took place during an unseasonably hot 105 degree hot and humid summer night.

The reception was well-catered while most of the guests would have appreciated cool salads, cool melons and tall cool drinks instead of grilled steaks and lemon chicken. The Dream Goddess's parents, unlike most proud parents of the bride, avoided all contact with the Prince's family and their guests for the entire evening. On one rare occasion, the bride's father and my best friend were standing right next to one another at the bar waiting for the bartender to fill a drink request. The bride's father deliberately turned his back towards and faced away from my friend and never spoke to or acknowledged that he even recognized the woman that had given birth to the man who had just married his daughter. The only time during the entire weekend festivities that the bride's father willingly engaged in a conversation with my friend and her husband was during the wedding rehearsal dinner the night before. That fact seeking conversation on behalf of the bride's father lasted an entire five minutes. You see, the Dream Goddess's father had quickly determined that my friend's family didn't travel in the same social and economics circles that he traveled.

And what about the bride's mother, you might ask? Well, the lady was less talkative and visible than her husband. She managed only to spend time with and to talk to her six sisters and other close family members that attended the reception/dinner. To be fair, to the bride's mother had a host of other relatives that attended the affair. So, the early warning signs of a pending disaster were demonstrated that day and evening; it was clear that the groom and his family were unacceptable to the bride's family. In addition to her family being distant to the Prince's family the bride spent her time at the reception with her cousins rather than lavishing any affection on the Prince or even attempting to make the Prince's family feel welcome. What an odd way to begin a lifetime with a man to whom the Dream Goddess had pledged undying love, loyalty and fidelity to just a few short hours before.

The hot heat of sexual desire that surrounded the courtship of the Prince and the Dream Goddess was actually a metaphor for the Prince's life. The young Prince had lived most of his life believing that he had been abused and deprived, intentionally, when he was a child by his family. The Prince mistakenly thought that his new wife's family would give him everything that he felt that he had missed and deserved in life. Ah, how wrong can youth be? For the Prince couldn't have been more mistaken in his belief that: he had clearly jumped from a perceived frying pan into a very searing, fire.

My friend's family and I departed the festivities and returned to our hotel rooms for a bit of respite and relief from the heat. For me, because of my attachment to my friend, I knew that the huge tragedy that was looming for her son would ultimately break her heart. Like most mother's who love their sons, my friend simply wanted her son to meet and marry a decent and caring woman one day who would, in the process of life, love him completely and selflessly. But of course we are all too familiar with the fact that all dreams and prayers just aren't answered. And as surely as night follows day, it was clear that my friend's fervent prayer had been surely missed or misheard by the Man in charge. The Prince's hopes about being totally accepted by his wife's family also went unfulfilled. Instead, the Prince's hopes and dreams were shot down by the Dream Goddess and her clan. The Prince's crushed dreams floated back to earth like singed butterflies after being caught in an intense fire. After the stupendous wedding day the Prince faded into obscurity in the lives of the Dream Goddess and her clan. The Prince was transformed into and only became a tarnished symbol that was to be ignored or ridiculed.

After marriage, the Dream Princess became known as the Toothy Goddess in my friend's household. To make a very sad and heart wrenching story short, the Toothy Goddess ended up breaking the Prince's heart and she may have possibly destroyed the very best parts of his soul and spirit.

It wasn't very long before my friend and her daughters began to understand why they had all been so standoffish and watchful of the Toothy Goddess. Shortly after the wedding, the Toothy Goddess began to expose her true colors to the Prince and his family. The Toothy Goddess was a proud and masterful manipulator who was also extremely selfish with a strong predilection for meanness that was obvious and difficult to misinterpret. The first sign of the decline: The Dream Goddess never ordered copies of their wedding photos nor did she send "Thank You" notes to the people who had given them gifts.

Needless to say the Prince's dream ended in much the way that it had began. A typically huge clan celebration took place at the Toothy Goddess's parents' home to celebrate Christmas Eve. Even before the marriage, the Toothy Goddess demanded the Prince only attend holiday functions at her family's home. After the wedding, the Prince's family became inconsequential to her plan therefore my friends' family and their feelings were unimportant to Toothy Goddess and her clan. To mollify his bride, the Prince acquiesced to her demands, believing that she would mellow and agree to attend functions at his family's home in the future. To put it simply, she never mellowed.

The Prince's family was never invited to any of the Toothy Goddess's family gatherings but I am certain that if an invitation had been offered my friend probably would have graciously declined. Anyway, after the young children, which included my friend's grandson, were given their gifts the adults exchanged gifts with one another. The Toothy Goddess and the Prince returned to their modest two bedroom apartment with their son. The two had barely entered the front door of their home when the Toothy Goddess decided that it was high time for her to shed a little light on her recent behavior to the Prince. The Toothy Goddess began by explaining her extended absences from their home. Although she claimed to be in school or in the library studying, the Toothy Goddess was plotting her exit from the marriage. Consumed with fire and brimstone, the Toothy Goddess frothed at the mouth as she informed the Prince that she no longer wanted to live with him; that the marriage was over, and to get out. The Toothy Goddess threw the Prince out of their home on a very bleak Christmas Day.

As the Prince slunk away in shame from the Dream Princess and his son with his paltry belongings he somehow missed the broad Cheshire cat grin that spread across the Toothy Goddess's face as he left. After months had passed it became clear that the Toothy Goddess had planned her whole exit from the relationship and she was overjoyed to be back in the bosom of her family without the burden of the Prince. The Toothy Goddess desired to return to her parent's home but not in shame; therefore she found an acceptable young man to marry and once her position had been completely re-cemented with her family and she had re-gained access to her numerous trust funds, the ruse of getting pregnant and living with someone obviously beneath her station in life became unnecessary. For the Toothy Goddess, alone with her infant son, on that bleak Christmas night was a night indeed to be celebrated. As the Toothy Goddess dozed with sugar plums dancing in her head, she could not help but to mouth: Mission accomplished! How's that for chutzpah?

But all too often, many goddesses will often use their smiles to manipulate others and/or situations. The smile of the goddess is rarely used to impart warmth or even to convey nervous discomfort like other women who use their smiles. Most women use their smiles to instinctively dispel ill will or to defuse tense situations. Most women have a penchant for a nervous giggle whenever they are uncomfortable. The nervous laugh, in a staggering number of women, is meant to mask their fear or insecurity. The fear and/or insecurity is typically conveyed in a woman by the slight quiver of the lip that is supposed to release their built-up inner tension that builds when a woman is placed in an awkward circumstance.

On the other hand, the goddess/diva uses her smile to almost always disarm others such as their husbands, other men, and of course female adversaries. Think back to people who are revered Goddesses or masters of "the smile" such as the current high- profile Anne Coulter, Katie Couric or Nancy Grace. Close your eyes and recall from memory exactly how their smiles begin to form just before they launch a vitriolic attack against a perceived enemy. The lines on the edges of their faces begin to soften ever so slightly as their eyes twinkle and the muscles in their faces strain against the demand to smile despite their desire to grimace. These women are masters of subterfuge and manage to convey in a smile that deep emotional pool of disgust and revulsion that resides just under the surface of their smiles. A goddess can manage to force the edges of their mouths upwards in an attempt to fain friendliness while at the same time presenting their adversary an infectious girlhood smile while they relentlessly attack and eviscerate whoever may be their current prey.

How could a truly empathetic and caring woman attack the wives of the firemen who lost their lives at the World Trade Center? Apparently Ann Coulter will never be nominated for the Nobel Peace Prize because she attacks without emotion while using that little girl smile to deliver her vile attacks against undeserving targets. Every femme fatale in the movies has used "that smile" just before they mortally wound an adversary who clearly faces peril despite that disarming smile. I am certain that Marie Antoinette smiled beatifically before speaking those famous words: "Let them eat cake!"

Goddesses are far too capable of wielding ill will against anyone that crosses their paths. But many goddesses are born with or acquired a mean steak that courses through their dark hearts like the life blood that powers the rest of us. Once a practicing goddess has drawn blood it is impossible for them to suppress a desire to emotionally devastate another person. Goddesses not only delight in the moment of the attack against an adversary but goddesses, like animals, are drawn to those people and situations where they can publicly embarrass and humiliate them.

So, unless you intimately know the heart of the woman smiling warmly in your direction: Beware and approach with caution.

I Am Beautiful
Chapter 10

The goddesses of the world have a unique perspective on female physical beauty. Unlike most women, goddesses are physically self-assured and believe that they are the epitome of female physically perfection. If the goddess isn't the epitome of feminine perfection then she will pay tens of thousands of dollars to ensure her physical perfection.

Most men are probably baffled by this newsflash: all women are much more judgmental about theirs and other women's bodies than any man can ever imagine. Of course every man has an acceptable standard of beauty that he would prefer to exist in the women in his life but men also have sexual ideals that may be very different from their acceptable standard of beauty. The bottom line is that men and women view women's bodies very differently. Many men just appreciate the female form along with all of their differences and so-called imperfections. Far too many women are concerned with projecting to the world what they perceive is a perfect body and that idealized form is something that most women never achieve, even artificially.

Of course there are men, rich and poor, who are only attracted only to the "trophy woman." At the other end of the scale are men who are repulsed by "large" women while some men exclusively seek relationships with plus size women. All in all, most men are primarily interested in and attracted to women whether they are short, tall, slim, voluptuous, or drop-dead gorgeous. Most men simply find women, all women physically appealing and desirable. In contrast, women stand in front of the mirror to dissect and compare their bodies to the air-brushed female physical icons that appear in male magazines or even in female fashion magazines. A man can look at a woman and see that perfect swell of hips and a woman will interpret that same swell as - that woman has broad or wide hips and those hips sit on top of cottage-cheese thunder thighs. As sexual beings, a man's sexual turn-ons just so happens to be tied to his visual cortex and as such a man's sexual desire can be satisfied by women from every ethnic background and physical type.

Of course some men are highly critical and judgmental about whether or not their woman has what he considers an ideal body type. Even though the modern Feminist Movement has been in full swing for over forty years, women, even feminists spend a lot of time and money on their physical appearances. Believe it or not, there are still a lot of men in the world who prefer only to be involved with brainless women. Most men who find a certain woman attractive would also probably find it very difficult to turn down a sexual invitation from a sex goddess. Conversely, if a Brad Pit or a young Paul Newman propositioned a normal woman, she would simultaneously feel intrigue and possible titillation by the suggestion but right alongside those emotions would be her rising doubts about her perceived physical flaws. As quick as a wink, the proposition from the prime male would result in the woman smiling that uncomfortable smile as she makes a quick exit. If men ever wondered why women like to make love in the dark, here's another newsflash: it's so you can't see our flaws!

Women don't just dress to attract male attention but women dress to impress other women and to avoid female criticism. Even though men are clearly visual beings most would still be shocked to learn that women judge their own bodies and other women's bodies quite differently than men do. Unless a man stops and takes the time to listen to a woman he'll never hear the constant running commentary that normally takes place in a woman's head about other women's bodies and how they're dressed or should be dressed. And women constantly make comments about all the women in their lives whether they are women that they see in their immediate environment or women that they see in movies or on television. What men fail to realize or comprehend is that very early in life in a woman's life most little girls that manage to mature into women find something wrong with their bodies. The something wrong is usually something that no man would ever consider a physical failing. The physical failings that women usually obsess about range from beasts that are too small or too large to hips that are too narrow or broad or possibly a non-existent or too large butt and don't forget about those skinny, stick-thin legs or thunder thighs. Each one of these "flaws" to women represents a physical imperfection that promises to doom them from finding true love much less her knight in shining armor.

The sad fact is that most women carry some type of insecurity about their bodies, although most learn to suck it up and face the world, everyday, just the way God made them. But the goddesses aren't normal, physical women. Goddesses are self-assured and every goddess knows that she is a paragon of physical beauty.

To be sure, goddesses use their physical self-assurance to belittle other women. Every woman knows and understands all too well that how they look and what men consider physical perfection are a very large part of their daily consciousness. Yes, I'm quite aware of the feminist revolution but I am also aware that when liberated young women finish hopping into and out of bed with promising one night stands, most wake- up in the morning wondering if one of their many physical flaws would prohibit this one night stand from becoming something real and permanent.

Just take a look at all of those high-powered women who man, sorry, no pun intended, the District Attorney Offices, all the women doctors and scientists and the legions of professional women who go off to work everyday wearing high heels and chic suits and dresses to work. Add to this mix, the over-the-top success of "Sex in the City" and "Desperate Housewives." These shows are popular with women, not men because the female stars live glitzy, exciting lives and they always look sexy and fantastic. Unlike the real daily life experience of a lot of younger and older women, the women in "Sex in the City" and "Desperate Housewives" attract male attention even though those experiences were transient at best.

Goddesses, or the inherently beautiful ones, aren't quite so bothered by having to step-up their physical appearance just to compete in a competitive world where there are demonstrably more women than men. Like so many of the traits that are formed when little girls are very young, unquestioned and accepted standards of beauty are another one of those traits that little girls learn from their mothers and as teens, from their peers. What is 'acceptable' to other women as a cultural standard of beauty is a standard heeded by women long before they receive compliments about just hoe beautiful they are from their boyfriends, significant others or their husbands. Although a lot of little girls grow-up being their daddies pretty little princesses many of these girls enter adulthood with doubts about their physical beauty because of our air-brushed, beauty driven culture. Most mothers manage to laugh-off that minor sting of rejection they feel whenever their husbands fawn over their daughters in a father's need to fulfill his little darling's every wish.

Something happens to men when they become fathers and especially so to men who become fathers of little girls. Once upon a time there was a man who married a woman, a woman that he truly loved. After several years of wedded bliss the couple decided that it was time for them to consider starting a family. The two engaged in many conversations before they actually decided to undertake the task. There were a few issues that they couldn't agree upon, such as: 1.) he wanted a girl to be their first born and 2.) she of course wanted a boy to be her first born because she had been an only child and had always dreamed about having an older, protective brother. As the couple's desire for children increased the issue of whether to have a girl or a boy first, waned. To move the story along, let's suffice it to say that the lady in question became successfully impregnated. The question of what the sex of the future child would be became an unimportant issue because the wife was burdened with 'morning sickness' all day, everyday and all night, every night until she delivered their cherub.. The only time the poor mother-to-be didn't suffer from the up-chokes was soon after, like minutes, the delivery of their beautiful, new baby.

The couple wanted the very best for their new off-spring therefore they elected to pursue home delivery, at the time, a popular new-age, enlightened way to birth a healthy and happy baby. They practiced those breathing exercises (The Lamaze Method) relentlessly while the father to-be ruthlessly pinched the inside of his beloved wife's inner thigh to simulate the pain that she would experience during childbirth.

When the big day arrived, the mother-to-be was exhausted due to several reasons. First, the natural explosion of hormones in her body that signaled her child would soon present itself to the world and, second, those hormones sent her on a cleaning spree that lasted for hours. Exhausted but satisfied, the poor mom to-be fell asleep on their living room couch only to be jarred awake by a single gut-wrenching, off the Richter scale contraction. That memorable contraction struck at three in the morning. A hasty call was placed to the two doctors scheduled to deliver her baby at home. Exhausted but coping, the mom-to-be weathered the rest of the contractions and the doctors arrived at five in the morning.

After a quick examination by one of the two doctors, a gruff, but heart of gold female, inform the mom-to-be that she would manually break her still intact bag of waters. With a quick whip of the doc index finger the waters rushed out and the mom to-be and her husband were sent down the three flights of stairs to the park below to walk to hasten the dilation of her cervix. The two doctors watched the progress of her contractions from the balcony while sipping cups of hot, black coffee. Once her contractions reached a fever pitch, the mom-to-be could only withstand the discomfort of the contractions on all fours. Once the contraction passed, she was able to stand up and walk a few more paces. The balcony lounging docs signaled the young couple that it was time for them to return to their apartment doe the delivery. The extremely concerned husband and the exhausted mom-to-be retraced their steps back to their apartment. A mobile delivery table was set-up and waiting in their living room. In between contractions, sitting upright on the delivery table with her legs bent and pulled towards her stomach the mom-to-be was permitted to drink large gulps of orange juice to quench one of her recently developed cravings.

At some point during the delivery, the attending female doctor asked the husband if he would like to observe the physical progression of his soon-to-arrive offspring. As soon as the man had time enough to peer between his wife's legs he saw what he perceived to be his baby's head, mind you, a head that was still buried deep within his wife's birth canal. Squinting and peering into the small opening the proud to-be father announced: "It's a girl!" The female doctor snorted and asked why he thought his progeny would be a girl. He responded excitedly: "There's a curl on the top of her head!" The doctor snorted again and got back to the job at hand.

In less than forty-five minutes the proud father had the pleasure of catching his daughter as she exited her former home in a powerful shot. Not only did she enter the world with a head full of curly hair her entrance into the world sealed a lifelong love affair between the two. The child was not only precocious in her physical beauty but she was also physically gifted and the little princess grew and literally became her father's beating heart. There was absolutely nothing that the man could deny her. Whatever her little heart desired and even things that she had never thought about wanting, her proud daddy found a way to fulfill her every wish. At a very early age, the young princess adopted her mother's love for succulent lobster while her younger brother and her friends were quite ecstatic only about McDonald's Happy Meals, hamburgers, chicken nuggets or pizza.

The young princess turned seven a few months before her mother's birthday. Much like every other day since the birth of his little princess, the tired but proud father arrived at home from work with a package tucked securely under his arm. Once the curly headed princess heard her father's keys in the door, she sprang to her feet and ran to the door to see what surprise her father had bought for her that day.

On this special day the dad man held the gift of a giant lobster tail. In truth, the lobster tail had been purchased for his wife's birthday but the little princess whooped in delight as she happily ripped open the package. The father, unable to disappoint his precious princess, gifted the girl child with the gift he had purchased for his wife. Needless to say, his wife was more than a little bit annoyed and miffed after her daughter and asked her mother to cook the lobster for her. To add insult to injury, after the little princess had dined sufficiently on the sweet succulent tail and had drifted off into a blissful and satisfied sleep, the mom exposed her disappointment to her conflicted husband.

The husband, although shamed, threw off his wife's obvious disappointment and comments and shifted the blame to his wife by stating: "Oh, grow up. She's a little girl and you're supposed to be a grown woman!" For several weeks after this incident, the marital bed between the mom and dad was quite a chilly place indeed. For some reason, the man appeared to be completely unaware that he clearly placed his daughter and her desires above his wife's. Being male, he completely missed the fact that he was preparing his little angle to grow up and become an insufferable, selfish little girl who would one day be an unbearable woman, except in the eyes of dear old dad. This innocent relationship between a man and his daughter, the natural occurrence of a dad wanting to protect and lavish his little girl with the entire world, also sets in motion a series of future events that would surely turn his sweet little girl into a formidable, adult goddess.

But of course the saga of the princess and the dad didn't end on the father's egregious first faux pas. After graduating from high school the high-strung and impetuous, beautiful princess decided that she no longer needed the guidance of her mother and father and decided that she no longer needed to knuckle under to her parent's house rules and decided to move out on her own. When the young princess revealed her plans to her father, he was convinced that it was just idle chatter on her part, a spur of the moment decision based on the denial of some freedom. Being the main culprit in creating his daughter's spoiled mentality, the dad was aware of just how spoiled she had become over the years. He was also convinced that his princess wouldn't be stubborn enough to give-up the lifestyle that he provided for her. And of course, like so many other times in the past, the man was dead wrong.

One "dark and stormy night" after the tail end of another one of those monumental clashes that had become commonplace between the princess and her parents, the princess stormed out of the house with a pre-packed suitcase. Once the princess left hadn't returned home after a few hours the father went to look for her even though his wife told him to let the situation alone. A few stress-filled days passed with dear old dad losing sleep and relentlessly pacing the floors all because his little princess hadn't communicated with her parents since she left. The parents knew that she was alive and well because her younger brother had seen the princess since she escaped the nest and the princess, clearly luxuriating in her new-found freedom, invited her brother to visit her new apartment.

The revelation that his little princess wouldn't be returning home was so devastating to the man that he decided to also leave the family as well. Incredulous, but far wiser, the wife whipped her husband with a barrage of questions as he attempted to pack his belongings: "Are you aware of the fact that you have been married to me for almost a quarter century and almost a decade BEFORE she was born? And have you forgotten the fact that we still have two other children that deserve to have their father in their lives?" The man sat down, defeated, exhausted and clearly unable to reconcile his feelings of loss, betrayal and abandonment by the thing that he most adored as he weakly lamented to his wife: "So, just what am I supposed to do, now?" Stunned, the wife desperately tried heroically to contain the hot cauldron of anger that defined her very being at the moment, she began to pace and once calmed, sighed and finally stated: "Suck it up and understand that first of all she's your daughter and that she's supposed to grow-up and move away. If I recollect history correctly, you had no problem with me leaving my parents home to go off into the wide world with you when I was merely seventeen?" The man interjected weakly: "But that was different." The wife rolled her eyes heavenward and hissed: "Different how?" Tired and unwilling to listen to his disjointed logic, the wife waved her hand dismissively to stop a response that would surely place him into a deeper hole than he had already dug for himself on this issue: "Look, dear, the girl was merely born to us, a gift. Our job was to raise her so that she could go out into the world and survive on her own. It appears that she is fulfilling her destiny. Don't you think it's time that you let her go? Now get a grip and stop being an ass!"

If life were a fair deal, the man's infatuation with his princess daughter might have ended at that point. But of course life isn't fair and the man obviously needed to understand what his wife's father had felt when he gallantly swept her off her feet. After the princess had met her soon-to-be husband about ten years later although she had moved away years earlier she managed to visit her parents several times a week. But after this paragon of masculinity entered her life, the princess was unable to release herself from the dream long enough to see or hear anything except for that young man who had captured her heart. Her world was completely filled by her perfect, handsome young man, a fact that broke her father's heart.

Throughout all of her life the young princess had been a true physical beauty and as such she had almost always been surrounded by all sorts of adoring young men for many, many years. The broken relationship between the beauty and her father had mended and her father had begun to accept that his daughter's quest for freedom and independence was normal and did not threaten the bonds between them. After tasting freedom and proving that she was undeniably independent, the young lady resumed a healthy and full relationship with her parents and remained her father's favorite.

And then one day, the almost thirty year-old beauty brought home a special young man to meet her parents. The mother knew almost instantly that this young man was special and very different from all the rest of the young men her daughter had dated over the years. A year passed after the initial introduction and an odd restlessness gripped the princess, a sort of calm before the onset of a significant storm. The older and now mature princess who had once only been consumed with selfish pursuits now began to fawn on her younger sister and actually began to speak cordially to her younger brother. Magazines that catered to weddings and brides began to appear in her younger sister's bedroom which was odd because the younger sister didn't even have a boyfriend.

The ever patient wife received a breathless and almost inaudible telephone call one day from her eldest daughter's boyfriend. The young man called to offer a lunch invitation to the entire family. The young swain wanted them to join them at a nearby Dim Sum restaurant early Saturday afternoon. For those who don't understand "Dim Sum" just think Chinese smorgasbord on wheels.

The invitation was graciously accepted and the mom decided that a talk with her eldest was in order because she was certain that her daughter knew exactly why the young man had offered such a formal and cryptic invitation. The mom sat down with her daughter in what had previously been her daughter's bedroom: "So, what's the deal? Why did Paul call and ask us out to lunch rather than telling you to have us show up?" The princess fidgeted briefly, ducked her head and couldn't resist flashing her mom with her perfect and brilliant smile: "Mom. He's going to ask dad for my hand in marriage!" The mother hugged her daughter and bussed her cheek before leaving the room to contemplate just how severe the coming storm would affect the tranquility of her home.

The popular Cantonese restaurant was packed. There were at least three hundred hungry people that filled every available table and people were busy eating, pointing at and stopping passing food-carts filled with tantalizing foods that would satisfy every palate.

Paul was unusually quiet and having sensed his discomfort the mom began to tell anecdotal jokes about the princess and her childhood antics of being the family monkey. The princess loved hanging from the canopy of her crib when she was less than six months old. She also walked, independently at five months old. The mom's calm and embracing recitation seemed to also calm Paul's nerves a bit but the moment of truth arrived when the dessert carts began to circle the room.

Paul nervously cleared his throat and croaked: "Ah, Mr. Smith…" With every spoken word the volume of his voice decreased and at some point became almost inaudible: "Sir, I want to thank you for allowing me to date your daughter and to meet and spend time with your family." He paused nervously. "But sir, I'd like to ask for your permission to expand our relationship…." Giant pause. The air was so thick that it became difficult for Paul to breathe. It seemed as if everyone in the restaurant had stopped to listen in on this special conversation. The roar of silence filled Paul's ears. Paul labored to continue as the princess looked deeply into his eyes: "So sir, I would like to ask your permission to marry your daughter?" The mature princess looked expectantly at her father and her father stared back at her and frowned in bewildered confusion.

The wife beamed and her husband committed yet a greater faux pas by responding to Paul and in part to his daughter with: "Have you talked to Stephanie about this?" Paul appeared to sulk as the beautiful princess Stephanie launched herself at her father's throat. The wife responded quickly and arrested her daughter's attempt to assassinate her father on the spot by kicking her husband, forcefully, as she whispered violently in her husband's ear: "Say, yes! She's thirty years old. It's about damn time." Stunned, hurt and really not up to having to suffer his daughter's wrath, the father shook his head up and down to signal his assent. The beautiful young woman became even more beautiful as the glow from her joy spread. She couldn't contain herself as she bolted from her chair and flew to her father, encircling his bent and defeated head with her arms as she kissed him lightly on the top of his graying head: "Thank you daddy! Oh, thank you so much! You don't know how happy you have made me!" Tears began to form in her father's eyes as he whispered: "But there are so many things that you and I haven't done together yet! Now we'll never be able to do those…" and the words caught in his throat as he tried to stifle a heart breaking sob.

Relieved, Paul retrieved the bill and paid quickly. The two young lovers, completely unaware of the rest of the world left the group without even saying "goodbye." The dad was unaware that the two had left because he was transfixed by and wracked with pain as the tears fell freely down his proud features. It may be difficult to comprehend but the day that this dad had to give away his princess to another man was the hardest day of his life. His daughter's wedding day filled him with a sense of loss that was greater than the loss of innocence that he had endured as he fought in the killing fields of Vietnam.

Unlike other goddesses, the princess Stephanie had been raised by a very earth-bound woman who believed that girls had to be more than beautiful to be happy and successful in life. Although the princess Stephanie could be quite brash about her physical attributes, the princess Stephanie grew-up and became a hardworking and successful woman. Her husband is still madly in love with her physical attributes but he is also aware that what drives his love for is her inner beauty and character rather than her exterior beauty.

But the world is filled with beautiful women and many of them aren't aware of their physical beauty while others, meaning the goddesses, walk through life with a haughty expression on their finely sculpted features while intimidating and insulting other women. Goddesses ensure that mere mortal women understand that in the pecking order of life when competing for men, position and power that the playing field is clearly in the domain of the goddesses.

Epilogue
Chapter 11

The preceding ten chapters have focused on how women can be at their very worst. Truth be told, women can actually act a whole lot worse than what appears in the preceding pages. But this final chapter is actually dedicated to all the hard-working, underappreciated women who raise respectful and caring children and who also embrace the true concept of what it means to be a woman.

There have been many women who have been angels in my life. From the preceding pages it might appear that my life experience and the experiences of other women that I interviewed and shared life experiences with have all lived lives that have been woefully bereft of women who are supportive, kind and loving. The truth is that my life experience, like many of the women that I interviewed and spoke to about these issues also gifted me with stories of many healthy and wonderful relationships with other women. But the point of this book was to expose that small fraction of females who advocate, manipulate and plot only for their own well-being and have left the rest of us wondering about our own self-worth, value and place in the universe. And don't think for a moment that adult mean girls haven't left their mark on the lives of legions of other women. For the goddess class, part of the sport of the culture is to cause pain while inflicting soul-numbing insecurity in other women.

So, a nod becomes necessary to acknowledge all the women who will never be honored with an award or an expensive piece of jewelry or a trip to an exotic playground.

I'll begin by first acknowledging a few of the women who have crossed my path over the years. The first person that I thought that I would have never acknowledged in a positive way is my mother. My mother was a goddess/diva and I always somehow disappeared in the glare of her limelight. My mother was clearly a beautiful goddess who demanded that I and my father fulfill her every wish. But a few days ago, after talking with a distant cousin long-distance about our family and the past through the lens of the present, I was finally able to "see" the woman who had been my adversary for most of my life.

My mother was a strict disciplinarian and whatever I did, no matter how hard I tried, I was never quite good enough for her. The talk with my cousin brought to the surface information about my mother that she rarely talked about to me or to others about her childhood that was anchored in poverty and abuse because of her alcoholic father and ten siblings. The point is, my mother left her family when she was still a child herself, at sixteen. She moved into my father's parents' home and brought me into the world. My grandmother, my father's mother, taught my mother how to save money and the value of hard work. My mother returned to school and landed a job in a small mid-western town where women were expected to only get married, have kids and to perform domestic chores in other women's houses in order to earn additional income for the family.

My mother burned with the desire to become something more than what was expected of her. And I didn't realize, until recently, that she also worked hard to give me a chance to live a life that she could have only dreamed about. Oh, my mom missed the part about being the warm and fuzzy kind of mom who was always there to wipe away my tears and fears but she was the kind of mom who demanded that I always exhibit strength, a backbone and the necessity to persevere in the face of life's challenges.

So, finally "Thank You, Mom!"

Of course there are many other women who deserve kudos and recognition for being, sometimes more than just friends. So, to all the women who have managed to grow-up without being catty or a practicing "mean girl," Thanks and keep up the good work!

To all the women who have nurtured me along the way, and there have been many "Thank you!" And to all the women that I hope that this book will make a difference in your life....good luck and keep fighting the good fight!

About the Author

The writer has previously been published in the Los Angeles Times and is currently a contributor to Suite101.com. The writer is a wife, a mother, and a teacher. Her work career spans almost four decades and she has worked as both a line employee and as a manager in banking and education. Her favorite authors include Ray Bradbury, Sue Grafton and Walter Mosley to name a few.

www.ingramcontent.com/pod-product-compliance
Lightning Source LLC
Chambersburg PA
CBHW020912290526
45784CB00002BA/514